House Beautiful

Abrams, New York

House Beautiful
Live *Colorfully*

Joanna Saltz and the
editors of *House Beautiful*

CONTENTS

LIVE COLORFULLY

WELCOME!

I've always thought that one of the best jobs in the world is naming paints. *That yellow is just like a No. 2 pencil. This blue is exactly the color of a July sky.* Splashing one of these onto the walls of your home is like prepping the canvas of your life. "There's a reason we don't see the world in black and white," beloved designer Celerie Kemble once told *HB*. Wistful pastels, electric leafy greens, pigment-rich reds and blues, even inky blacks and blinding whites . . . the outdoors would be a very sorry place without them, so why would we settle for any less in our homes? Inside this book you'll find nearly one hundred homes awash in color, and probably your dream palette too. All credit to the designers. As anyone who's wielded a paintbrush knows, it's not very easy to whip up a vibrant and yet truly livable color palette. The experts employ infinite tricks: fabrics with a thousand dyes in the weave, trim defining the edge of a piece of upholstery, and (of course) very carefully selected paints. When you hear the word *color*, what do you feel? Thrill or trepidation; it's rarely something in between. But using it doesn't mean you have to paint all the walls chartreuse. So-called neutral tones can be appetizing: cream, cinnamon, coffee, nutmeg, almond. Gemstone tints, from emerald to ruby to amethyst, are rich and seductive but very much mined from the natural world. Or maybe you'd like to live in a watercolor painting? Pastels! Whichever palette suits your personality, the beauty of living colorfully is that whichever combination you choose, it will be completely unique.

—Joanna Saltz

LIVE COLORFULLY

Earth Tones

WOODSY BROWNS, SUNSET ORANGES, SANDY OCHERS. Earthy interiors channel the simple beauty of the natural world for a serenely grounding effect. They are quiet and calming but never boring; a breath of fresh air.

STUDIO SHAMSHIRI
Los Angeles

"When you get there, you don't want to leave."

"Everybody is using white oak, that's very much a thing of our time, so I try to avoid it as much as possible," says Shamshiri, who instead used black walnut paneling to tie this room to the kitchen cabinets. *Paint:* All White, Farrow & Ball. *Pendant:* Lisa Johansson-Pape. *Cushions:* custom, in mohair. *Table:* custom. *Chairs:* vintage Danish.

A Southern California hillside is a tricky place to set down roots: The sun leaves plantings in the dark half the year, and drought and fire are never far from mind. But this house in Los Angeles, a sunny nineties build on a sizable plot of land in Bel Air, inspired the homeowner to nest, and he called in his friend Pamela Shamshiri of Studio Shamshiri to handle the renovations. "I wanted it to be like a womb," the designer says. "It was really my goal for him to love this house and to be in it for a long time."

To that end, Shamshiri and her team overhauled the interiors, cloaking the home in soothing wood tones and blue-greens, and sumptuous textures to foster a cocooning effect. They chose California walnut for the extensive millwork, sourced vintage and custom furnishings to complement the client's private art collection, and tapped local Hollywood craftspeople to produce showstopping moments, like an aged copper bar. "We have one metalworker who's literally a lowrider guy, who has the right stuff because he does bumpers," says Shamshiri, whose background is in set design. "It all adds up to a narrative, so we are very precise with our material language."

Getting to that point was easier said than done, however. Several months into construction, it was discovered that the windows—a major selling point for the owner—had to be removed due to unresolvable water issues. "It was a big emotional loss for me," says Shamshiri, who made the most of the six-month delay by working out new metal window casings that felt stylistically in line with the house. These frame "a hillside of wildness" outside, designed by landscape architecture firm Terremoto.

"It's always been my inclination [to create] homes that are a place of refuge, because we're living in an era where you need that," says Shamshiri. "I used to say, 'You're gonna put your socks on and never want to leave!'"

(PREVIOUS) A buttery leather Hans Wegner armchair, burnished brass lighting, and a headboard upholstered in Ashbury Hides suede create a cocoon-like feel in the primary bedroom. *Sconce:* vintage. *Lamp:* vintage Lisa Johansson-Pape. *Nightstand:* custom walnut.

(ABOVE) Featuring an aged brass panel and raw copper countertop, the bar "felt so right for this house and this client," says Shamshiri, "subtle and sophisticated." *Millwork:* custom, Northstar Cabinet Construction. *Faucet:* Vola.

"It was really my goal for him to love this house and to be in it for a long time."

Black walnut shelving was built into the wall, rather than on top of it. *Paint:* For similar, try Down Pipe, Farrow & Ball. *Floor lamp:* Lisa Johansson-Pape. *Sofa:* Umberto Asnago for Arflex. *Chaise:* vintage Bruno Mathsson. *Coffee table:* Alma Allen. *Rug:* Mansour Modern.

HOW TO PAIR PAINTS
with Wood

—

"Juxtaposition is key when using multiple species of wood," says Shamshiri. Pair light and dark finishes for a distinctive look—just don't overdo it. "I like to keep species to one or two max, and I always use the same species on millwork throughout," says Shamshiri. Then, think of each wood grain as a color when you choose paints to pair with it—a dark blue-gray, like Farrow & Ball Down Pipe, plays off the dark grains in a rich walnut. "This blends the wood to read as a part of the palette more so than the overarching material," the designer explains.

15

(ABOVE) "I wanted to make sure the owner felt like he had a new cozy home base," says Shamshiri. *Paint:* Stiffkey Blue, Farrow & Ball. *Armchair:* vintage Marco Zanuso. *Cocktail table:* vintage Danish rosewood. *Rug:* Christopher Farr. *Console:* vintage André Sornay. *Art:* client's own.

(RIGHT) "My personal goal was to make a kitchen that would persuade him to cook," Shamshiri says. *Pendants:* vintage Hans-Agne Jakobsson. *Flush mounts:* Robert Lewis Studio. *Range:* Wolf. *Cabinetry:* custom, Northstar Cabinet Construction. *Counter stools:* Blackcreek Mercantile.

LIVE COLORFULLY

KURECK JONES
Martha's Vineyard, Massachusetts

Carefree colors, waterproof everything, and ocean views.

(PREVIOUS) "Painting the floor a consistent color neutralized it and united the whole space," says Kureck. Foscarini's Spokes 2 pendant, which maximizes the view by day, glows by night. *Floor paint:* Stone Blue, Farrow & Ball. *Table:* vintage travertine, Carlo Scarpa. *Chairs:* vintage, in Jerry Pair leather. *Art:* Joseph W. Reed.

(RIGHT) "We put windows in the corners for a full projection into the trees and the ocean beyond," says Jones. "You are in the treetops." *Sectional:* B&B Italia. *Throw pillows:* custom, made from vintage Japanese textiles. *Coffee table:* vintage, Paul Frankl. *Rug:* custom crochet, Nasiri Carpets. *Armchairs:* vintage.

Before the design and architectural firm Kureck Jones got to work on this Martha's Vineyard house, built in the early 2000s, it was the opposite of a breezy vacation home. "It was a dated warren of rooms, really dark and internal," says John Kureck.

As renters, the clients had loved the house for its right-near-the-water location, and they considered starting fresh by building instead of renovating. However, that would have taken an eternity: New construction is often a three-year process in these parts, not to mention the two-year permit wait to put in a swimming pool. (And all this was prior to pandemic delays.) So Kureck and his partner, Doug Jones, dug in, working with Holmes Hole Builders not for a simple nip and tuck but full-on reconstructive surgery. "We stripped it to the absolute," says Jones of the gut renovation that would yield an airier, beachy feeling. "We started from scratch."

The ultimate goal: Make the house brighter, more family-friendly, and better focused on the panoramic ocean views beyond. They moved the kitchen (it now opens out to the pool), added a screened porch, and replaced all *forty* of the home's small, old windows. Most of the main level's walls were then paneled in natural ash wood, and, since many of the contractors they hired were shipbuilders, the final effect is that of a boat's hull. "Even at night, the house has a sort of golden glow to it," Kureck says.

In a place this relaxed, you shouldn't have to cry over spilled mojitos. Kureck Jones opted for easily swept painted-wood floors and kitchen counters made of PaperStone, which is fabricated from compressed recycled paper and is essentially immortal. So, too, is the dining table, a Carlo Scarpa design from the 1970s made of solid travertine. The family even ordered an extra set of covers for the B&B Italia sofa in the living room, so that if a stain should befall one cushion, it could be replaced from the same dye lot.

Ingeniously, the pair used color to make the house feel brighter. "You can't paint a room white, and put white furniture in it, and automatically have it read as light," Kureck explains, pointing out the black-and-white flower artwork in the dining room and the inky fireplace base. "The trick to lightness is actually contrast." That blue floor that mimics the color of the ocean out the window? Hardly coincidence. It all reads as the summer home ideal—and that's just how the family likes it.

(PREVIOUS LEFT) "Everything here is mobile," Jones explains. And durable: The seats are covered in waterproof Ultrasuede "so you can plop down in your bathing suit." *Sofa and chairs:* Togo, Ligne Roset. *Coffee table:* Airborne International from 1stDibs. *Curtain fabric:* Hanami, Zak+Fox.

(PREVIOUS RIGHT) "We mounted window shades up to the ceiling, covering most of the walls and making the room read taller," Jones explains. *Ceiling fixture:* Marset. *Chairs:* Pottery Barn Teen. *Window shade fabric:* Jane Churchill for Cowtan & Tout.

(LEFT) A semi-open floor plan encourages mingling during meal prep. *Tile:* Fireclay Tile. *Chandelier:* vintage, Billings Auction. *Sectional:* Ray, B&B Italia. *Coffee table:* vintage, Paul Frankl. *Painting:* FX by Dan Christensen. *Rug:* custom crochet, Nasiri Carpets. *Armchairs:* vintage.

THE BEST PAINT FOR *Flooring*

—

Why should walls have all the fun? An unexpected painted floor can be the perfect blank canvas to reinvent any room. But if you're worried about pesky scratches and scuff marks, fear not: Armorseal Rexthane I by Sherwin-Williams is an industrial-strength high-gloss enamel with all the finesse of a boutique paint. "After an extensive search for the best white floor paint, this is the hands-down winner," raves designer Dan Mazzarini. "It's both durable and visually stunning, and it can be tinted to any color."

URSINO INTERIORS
Larchmont, New York

Carefully orchestrated details
make this home feel like a boutique hotel.

(PREVIOUS) To elevate the
more formal rooms in the front
of the house, Ursino chose a
deep green hue (Benjamin Moore
Topsoil) and added heavy wool
drapery by Castel Maison. "Using
earthy shades and organic
materials in simple forms brings
the design down to earth," she
says. *Sofa:* custom. *Coffee table:*
custom. *Rocking chair:* Design
Within Reach. *Lamp:* Currey &
Company.

Subtle green accents in the family
room's antique rug echo the wall
paint in other parts of the house.
A neutral backdrop of Benjamin
Moore Sheep's Wool, a Lawson–
Fenning chair and ottoman, and
a calacatta marble fireplace
surround have a serene energy.
Floor lamp: Circa Lighting. *Drink
table:* Katy Skelton.

It was the eleventh hour. But as Maureen Ursino stood in the newly framed kitchen of a Tudor home in Larchmont, New York, she'd been working on, she couldn't shake the feeling that the blue they had chosen for the cabinetry was all wrong.

"It was that classic case of what you plan for on paper isn't always what happens in reality," says Ursino, who collaborated with homeowners Dan and Jamie Bienstock and Jeff DeGraw of DeGraw & DeHaan Architects on the new build. "A lot of the other parts of the house had developed in a different direction, so the blue was [now] feeling like more of an outlier." DeGraw had his own color epiphany a few hours earlier: Instead of painting *just* the wood-beamed dining room green, the same sultry shade would be carried into the adjacent entryway and living room. These three formal rooms face the front of the house and give way to a more contemporary, bright kitchen and family room in the rear; unifying their color scheme emphasized the transition.

What made sense for the cabinets was a deep, soulful color to anchor the spaces; they landed on Tanner's Brown by Farrow & Ball. "That may have been the most stressful decision point of the whole project, but now I could never imagine the cabinets any other color," laughs Dan, who acknowledges that

he and his wife needed some convincing. As the chief people officer at EOS Investors, Dan honed his eye and attention to detail while working under Andrew Zobler, founder and CEO of the Sydell Group, the hospitality brand behind stylish boutique hotels like Nomad and Line. "I saw how colors and furniture and lighting can make you feel and thought, *Why not translate that to my home?*"

For DeGraw, that meant creating a line of continuity between the curved elements of the external architecture and the interior rooms. "There's a sensuous feel to the whole space," he says of walls that meet in parabolic curves instead of sharp angles. Ursino, for her part, ran with the idea in every detail, choosing bow-shaped cutouts in the custom legs of the kitchen island and a bullnose trim for a marble element on the range hood. She even extended that concept to the furnishings, a mix of refined yet approachable pieces clad in earthy, organic wools to soften the sense of formality.

"Dan said early on that he didn't want his house to feel like every other house you see," recalls Ursino. "So we zeroed in on all the details. Every decision was so carefully considered. All the small things made such a difference." Perhaps especially those last-minute swaps.

—

"There's a sensuous feel to the whole space."

(ABOVE) Ursino took her cues from English country homes for the second-floor kid's bathroom, which she distinguished with Farrow & Ball Pigeon (vanity) and Peignoir (walls). *Roman shade:* Carolina Irving. *Bench:* vintage.

(RIGHT) Exposed wood ceiling beams and classic wall paneling link the dining room to the Tudor-style architecture, but streamlined contemporary furnishings keep it feeling modern. *Pendant:* Articolo *Lighting.* Sconces: Materia. *Art:* Britt Bates. *Table and chairs:* custom.

LIVE COLORFULLY

ALEXANDER DOHERTY DESIGN
New York City

For a couple stuck in the neutral zone,
a duplex is reimagined in saturated tones.

(PREVIOUS) A faux-parchment wall treatment by Artgroove establishes a serene backdrop for the exploration of color in the living room, where a vintage Luigi Massoni games table mingles with chairs upholstered in Rogers & Goffigon leather and a velvet AERO bench.

(RIGHT) "To have a staircase in New York is quite exceptional," says Doherty. "I wanted to create a feeling of refinement." So he paneled the walls in cerused oak and added a custom Stark runner. *Stool:* vintage Jacques Adnet. *Pedestals and busts:* Gerald Bland.

"It wasn't about choosing the wildest colors. It was about creating visual interest."

Asking clients to step outside their comfort zones can be a tricky part of a designer's job. But when the roles are reversed and a client freely tasks *them* with pushing the limits, magic happens. Such was the case when one fashion-industry couple moved from a converted loft space in New York City to a characterless 3,800-square-foot duplex in a prestige building in the West Village. They gave designer Alexander Doherty carte blanche to engage in a little color shock therapy.

"The clients had always lived in a beige world," explains Doherty. "They wanted to experiment and try something they had never experienced before. I wanted to give them a real sense of departure, because when you employ someone to do something like this, that person *has* to give you something you wouldn't do for yourself. Otherwise, what's the point?"

It helped that the apartment's entry was dominated by a rare (for Manhattan) double-height foyer with floor-to-ceiling windows and a staircase, albeit a basic developer's option with what Doherty calls "dreary black metal spindles," that was one of the

first things to go. But the stage for drama was there—all the home needed was someone to bring in the showmanship.

Doherty did so with a mix of saturated hues that added richness and glamour to the boring white boxes. Cerused oak paneling and an espresso-painted ceiling create a cocooning effect in the entry; the coffee-inspired shade continues on the underside of the now curved stairway to maintain the room's continuity— an important detail, considering the adjacent room is upholstered in grass-green felt. When asked how that specific color found its way into the palette, Doherty shrugs it off. "Why not? It's not science, what we do. You have to demystify it a bit. I said, 'Do you like it? If you do, then let's do it.'"

Rich colors characterize the living room, where a pair of terra-cotta-hued sofas play off a jade cocktail table and burnt-orange poufs. "It wasn't so much about choosing the wildest colors we could," says Doherty. "It was more about creating visual interest. [The clients] are homebodies; they wanted a place where they could slouch around and really be comfortable but also feel inspired."

34

(PREVIOUS LEFT) A study in indigo, the guest room displays Doherty's preference for saturated color. Farrow & Ball Stiffkey Blue sets the tone, while a Chelsea Textiles bedside table and Holland & Sherry–upholstered bed complete the scene. *Lamp:* vintage Murano glass. *Console:* vintage. *Artwork:* Francis Bott.

(PREVIOUS RIGHT) The chocolatey hue on the ceiling in the entry extends to the underside of the stairway. *Paint:* Espresso Bean, Benjamin Moore. *Console:* vintage Milo Baughman. *Lamp:* Stephen Antonson. *Art:* Francis Bott.

(RIGHT) To give the living room an eclectic feel, Doherty paired Parisian flea market finds with rich textures. *Vases:* vintage Jacques Ruelland. *Throw pillow fabrics:* Holland & Sherry, Fortuny, and de Le Cuona. *Stools:* Aero.

LAUREN LIESS + CO
Pompano Beach, Florida

A bachelor's escape that
blends seamlessly with the landscape.

EARTH TONES

"I wanted it to feel as if the outdoors were beckoning you in every room of the house."

When Lauren Liess's cousin, a bachelor at the time, asked her to help design his massive home in Pompano Beach, Florida, his vision involved a dark, "seemingly Dracula-inspired mansion," Liess recalls. For a landscaper who loves entertaining and being outdoors, it made little sense. So to translate the concept to sunny South Florida, Liess took the classical forms and beautiful old villas her cousin was attracted to and gave them an airy spin, infusing the home with natural materials.

Most of the six-bedroom, ten-bathroom home (by architect John Lamb, with landscaping by Adam Baker of Broward Landscape) was already in place when Liess came aboard. She helped select finishes and materials throughout, forgoing moldings and adding barrel-vaulted ceilings made of Jerusalem stone in the dining room and wine cellar. Pecky cypress, a wood native to Florida, brings warmth to the kitchen islands and beams. The en suite bathroom's walls and the bar are crafted from custom concrete. Much of the flooring is antique limestone. "I wanted it to feel as if the outdoors were beckoning you in every room of the house," Liess says.

To bring depth and meaning to the large home, which is painted entirely in Snow White by Benjamin Moore, Liess filled it with endless antiques and vintage pieces that took years to amass. "We spent so many hours on FaceTime and in-person shopping at antiques places, scouring for cool one-of-a-kinds," she says. Mismatched antique Spanish chairs in the dining room help accommodate big, casual family meals.

The project was truly a labor of love—one Liess did in her free time. "My cousin is like a brother to me, so I loved having the comfort level to push back and force things I might normally let go," she says. Now she enjoys seeing the home in action: a place for impromptu get-togethers, family reunions, and even weddings for friends.

(OPENER) Antique plaster and carved stone pieces were collected over years to hang on the 30-plus-foot wall. *Table, chairs, pillows, and rug (top):* vintage. *Mantel:* antique. *Rug (bottom):* Fibreworks.

(PREVIOUS) Made of reclaimed stone from Israel, the barrel-vaulted ceiling was one of the client's non-negotiables. *Chandelier:* Currey & Company. *Table lamps:* Circa Lighting. *Sideboard:* Sarreid. *Paint:* Snow White, Benjamin Moore. *Table, chairs, and art:* antique. *Statue:* of John the Baptist, unknown sculptor.

(LEFT) Glass doors open completely onto the loggia, pond, and coconut grove. *Curtains:* Lauren Liess Textiles. *Floor lamp:* Lauren Liess & Co. *Sofa, pillows, and blanket:* Verellen. *Coffee table and rug (top):* vintage. *Rug (bottom):* Fibreworks.

LIVE COLORFULLY

HALDEN INTERIORS
Weehawken, New Jersey

For a recent widow,
a bright home spotlights good memories.

"She needed it to be a happy place," recalls designer Kesha Franklin, but this seemingly simple directive from a client belied a much more nuanced task. Franklin, the founder of New Jersey–based Halden Interiors, had been enlisted by a set of siblings to help their recently widowed mother renovate her new waterfront condo in Weehawken.

If anyone knew about new beginnings, it was the apartment's owner, Patricia Hunter-Bunyan, a psychoanalyst and grief counselor. "There was a very interesting dynamic of a healer seeking healing," says Franklin, who endeavored to "lift" the white-walled space to create a sophisticated backdrop for her client's large and meaningful art collection, a mix of works by Black contemporary artists and pieces picked up during extensive travels with her late husband. It was a challenge, the designer says, that aligned perfectly with her own design style: "I love to bring in color, but at the same time, my work is streamlined."

Meeting her client's emotional needs meant first tackling structural ones. "Two of my biggest frustrations with condo buildings like this are the lack of overhead lighting and storage," says the designer. To address the former, Franklin reimagined the home's lighting plan, adding recessed and decorative fixtures. High-shine finishes and mood-boosting yellow accents help further reflect light.

The setting complete, focus shifted to art. "Each artifact and picture displays our rich history, tradition, and culture of the past," explains Hunter-Bunyan of her collection. Together, she and Franklin selected two dozen pieces to display in a back hallway, turning the passage into a private museum. When Hunter-Bunyan saw the finished gallery, Franklin recalls, she burst into tears—the happy kind. It was a fitting end to their journey: "It was an emotional project," says the designer. "We figured out who she was in this space."

(PREVIOUS) The client uses this guest bedroom to catch up on reading. *Nightstand:* Hooker Furniture. *Sconce:* Kelly Wearstler for Circa Lighting. *Pillows:* Ryan Studio and Piper Collection. *Wallcovering:* Zinc Textile. *Rug:* Safavieh. *Painting:* TAFA.

48

A painting by Robert Robinson hangs above a Nathan Anthony sectional and a one-of-a-kind coffee table from Nigeria. *Pillow fabric:* S. Harris (orange) and Calvin Klein Home. *Side table:* Interlude Home. *Lamp:* Arteriors. *Wallcovering:* Elitis. *Rug:* FJ Kashanian.

(LEFT) Pieces from the client's art collection—Nigerian Nupe pots, an acrylic work by H. Porter, and masks from Nigeria (top) and the Ivory Coast (bottom)—pop against Phillip Jeffries grasscloth. *Stools:* Bernhardt.

(ABOVE) It's sunny skies 24/7 with Omexco Sisal Sunflower wallpaper on the ceiling. *Chandelier:* Apparatus Studio. *Table:* Nuevo Living. *Chairs:* Nathan Anthony with Theodore Alexander fabric.

ERIN SANDER DESIGN
Dallas

Clean materials and a kid-friendly palette
give this home an easygoing air.

"We essentially inverted the palette by bringing the teak wood flooring—seen in the primary bathroom—to the exterior and placing the polished concrete indoors," says Sander. "Often you have the wood tones overhead, but here we've put it underfoot." An additional sunken seating area off the dining room offers extended entertaining space. *Concrete fire box:* custom, Brian Sarché Concrete Design. *Coffee table:* custom teak. *Pillows:* Kufri. *Seating:* client's own.

"Above everything else, we wanted it to be unique." When Texas custom home builder Ben Coats was contemplating the finishing touches for his home in Dallas's coveted Bluffview neighborhood, he knew the interiors needed to resonate with both the architect's Hamptons-style design *and* his young family's lifestyle. After consulting with interior designer Erin Sander on another client's property, Coats hired her to deliver on his family's vision.

With five young children to consider, Sander's first priority was comfort. The designer began by choosing a color palette forgiving to kids (lots of rich neutrals, like polished concrete floors), then layered in plenty of casual elements with "some great high and low moments," like chairs from Urban Outfitters paired with a bespoke sofa in the living room. At the same time, the home had to be something of a showplace, considering the owner's occupation. Sander explains: "Ben needs to use his home as a calling card for his business."

"It's next level," Coats says with a laugh. "Our passion is clean living, so it was important that we used all-natural materials as much as possible." While untreated, unstained cedar shingles cover the home's exterior, polished concrete, locally sourced white oak, and native post oak—also unstained—present a natural, soothing feel inside. "These materials wear nicely, and we wanted the house to be a little rugged that way."

(PREVIOUS) A custom-built, steel-clad marble floating fireplace separates the family's main gathering space from the dining room. "The custom bench serves as the hearth—it's a place where the family gathers in the evenings to read or relax," says Sander. *Mixed-wood chair and woven stool:* Palecek. *Orange chair:* Hickory Chair. *Bench:* Lee Industries. *Side table:* Stahl + Band. *Console table:* Made Goods. *Light fixture:* Modish Store.

"These materials wear nicely,
and we wanted the house to be
a little rugged that way."

LIVE COLORFULLY

(LEFT) Disconnected from the public spaces by a hallway for maximum privacy, this bedroom is an airy retreat for the busy couple. *Bed:* Anthropologie. *Nightstands:* custom, the CEH. *Rug:* Loloi. *Lighting:* Brendan Bass. *Bell art:* MQuan Studio.

"Outdoor showers aren't necessarily unique if you live in Malibu—but they are for Dallas," explains Coats. "We custom built this steel shower that protrudes from the house, so you feel like you're outside." *Rug:* Minna Home.

Blue

(01)

If you could bottle a feeling
of calmness, this is what it would look like.

(02)

(03)

(04)

(01) Designer Aamir Khandwala chose a custom semicircle sofa inspired by Milo Baughman for this living room. *Light:* custom. *Floor lamps:* vintage, Pamela Lerner Home & Design. (02) By coating every surface in this kitchen in Benjamin Moore Sea Serpent, a rich blue, designer Melanie Millner made it feel limitless. *Range hood, cabinetry, and island:* custom, Kingdom Woodworks. *Stools:* Hellman-Chang. *Chandelier:* Jonathan Browning Studios. (03) The Fox Group's Cara Fox used Old Navy, Benjamin Moore (and custom 24-carat gold drawer pulls!), to distinguish this butler's pantry. *Shade fabric:* Schumacher. *Sink:* Shaws. (04) Bella Mancini translated her client's love of color with International Klein Blue chairs and a white Saarinen table on the enclosed porch.

(06)

(07)

(05) A gallery wall of vintage mirrors, all painted Farrow & Ball Pitch Black, pop against the Grow House Grow wallcovering in this powder room by Cecilia Casagrande. *Vanity:* Kallista. (06) Designer Caitlin Wilson went with Benjamin Moore Pike's Peak Gray, an understated French Blue, in her mudroom. *Wallcovering:* Lee Jofa. *Shade fabric:* Caitlin Wilson. *Marble floor tile:* Paris Ceramics. (07) Graphic tiles and cheerful blue cabinetry give this kitchen by Caren Rideau a strong point of view. *Cabinetry:* Caren Rideau. *Tiles:* Veranda Tile Design. (08) To modernize her vacation home while lending it a sense of nostalgia, designer Heidi Caillier painted the 1970s wall paneling Farrow & Ball Down Pipe. *Armchairs:* Rejuvenation, upholstered in Ralph Lauren plaid. *Table:* Jayson Home. (09) Designer Noz Nozawa updated a midcentury kitchen with Shaker-style cabinetry and a crisp blue-and-white theme. *Backsplash:* Fireclay Tile. *Pendants:* Arteriors.

(08)

(09)

5 DESIGNER-APPROVED
Blue Paints

—

"Evoke the ocean's mysterious depths with Benjamin Moore Venezuelan Sea."

—

JAMIE DRAKE & CALEB ANDERSON, co-founders of *Drake/ Anderson*

"We love using Benjamin Moore Woodlawn Blue on the ceiling to give the space a sense of endlessness."

—

MEG RODGERS, principal of *Marguerite Rodgers*

"I love Farrow & Ball Hague Blue for its intrinsic quality of timelessness. It is elegant and sophisticated."

—

MICHAEL COX, founder & principal of *Foley & Cox*

"Farrow & Ball Stone Blue works with other warm colors because of the little bit of red it has, and really sings when used with a high-gloss finish."

—

KATIE RIDDER, principal of *Katie Ridder*

"Ressource Peintures Noir Encre is a sultry indigo with a depth of color that comes from a unique application of multiple undercoats."

—

RODNEY LAWRENCE, principal of *Rodney Lawrence Inc.*

(10)

(10) The cabinetry in this Phoebe Howard–designed kitchen is a color match of the custom Peter Fasano gingham, cut 50 percent. *Shades:* Joss Graham. *Sconces:* Hector Finch. *Tile:* Crystal White, Mediterra. *Faucet:* Dornbracht. *Sink:* Rohl. *Hardware:* Martel Hardware.

(11)

(12)

(13)

(11) Cerused oak cabinetry, reclaimed barnwood beams, brass accents, and a soothing blue—Normandy by Benjamin Moore—impart a nautical feel to this kitchen by Meredith McBrearty. *Tiles:* Waterworks. *Pendant:* The Urban Electric Co. (12) A brass Circa Lighting chandelier adds a bit of sparkle in a bathroom by Clara Jung of Banner Day Interiors. (13) Designer Nina Magon gave this sitting area a sense of elegance with Sherwin-Williams Seaworthy. *Chairs:* CB2. *Square ottoman:* Molteni.

LIVE COLORFULLY

Primary Colors

RED, BLUE, and YELLOW are more than
just child's play—they will turn any space into a
work of art, and they're also mood boosters.

ORE STUDIOS
Seattle

One designer found the potential in his client's home by looking up.

LIVE COLORFULLY

(PREVIOUS) Beers describes the cantilevered room in this home as "a large transparent jewel box that hangs over the forest floor. Seating is configured around a mass fireplace—a kind of campfire, in a sense." *Pillows:* custom, Ore Studios, in Kvadrat fabric. *Blue chair:* Eero Saarinen, Knoll. *Wood chair:* vintage, Folke Ohlsson for Dux. *Side table:* CB2. *Coffee tables:* Blu Dot. *Rug:* custom Moroccan, Paulig.

This kitchen has one of the few exposed lighting fixtures in the house, a Lindsey Adelman piece for Roll & Hill. *Table:* Montis. *Chairs:* vintage, Inco of California, in Knoll felt. *Paint:* White Dove, Benjamin Moore. *Cabinetry:* custom, Kerf Design. *Tile:* Ann Sacks. *Counter stools:* Muuto. *Range:* Wolf. *Wall ovens:* Bosch.

"There's something poetic about putting these angular shapes in the middle of nature," says Andy Beers, the principal designer of Ore Studios. Set against the backdrop of a bluff overlooking Puget Sound, the modern facade of his latest creation, a new build by DeForest Architects, is the stuff of movie magic: Cantilevered glass common rooms jut into a canopy of hundred-year-old trees, with private quarters tucked into the hillside.

The home's owners, a graphic designer and a fine artist, spend as much time outside with their kids as they can. "They wanted a home that was both tranquil and surprising," Beers says. Huge black windows frame wooded views and give way to rooms with pale bleached floors, dark cabinets, and white walls. By contrast, the furnishings are both elegant and cheeky, a mix of modern pieces from brands like Knoll, Blu Dot, and CB2 plus independent makers. More than one cocktail table is covered in black-and-white Beetlejuice stripes.

The wife felt anchored to certain materials and colors from the outset: "It was always going to be primaries," Beers says. "Blue came into the project when she brought stoneware passed down by her aunt to the first meeting." This collection is now proudly displayed in the kitchen, where asymmetrical wood cabinets feature the occasional red panel to reference the living room rug. Since the main level is open, all of the rooms needed to work together; a tight palette was used throughout. Beers opted for less-saturated versions of the colors used in the common rooms for a calming but continuous design. "A pale blue rug and patterned settee are small departures from the solid blocks of color used downstairs," he says of the main bedroom.

Branching off from the central area are escape routes to hidden nooks with dramatic views and comfy seating. In addition to creating a sense of adventure, says Beers, these "allow for the connected public spaces to stay tidy." Everywhere you turn, there's a cozy room overlooking the woods or the water, the designer says. "It almost feels like an island retreat."

69

(ABOVE) "The stair assembly responds to the geometry of the house," says Beers. *Design:* DeForest Architects. *Light:* Ecosense. *Paint:* Chili Pepper, Benjamin Moore.

(RIGHT) Beers carved out a quiet space for the homeowners to focus on work and such, "so those things don't creep into the public rooms." *Shelving unit:* Blu Dot. *Desk:* Kerf Design. *File cabinets:* Poppin. *Chair:* vintage, Eames for Herman Miller.

LIVE COLORFULLY

MARK D. SIKES
Marin County, California

How a preppy color scheme gave this light-filled
landmark home new life.

"It's just a really special little jewel." That's how designer Mark D. Sikes describes this family home. Set atop a hill in Marin County, California, the 1925 house had great natural light and good bones—and was designated a historic landmark. Practically speaking, this means "the front of the house and the size of the house can't really be changed, but internally, you're able to do pretty much whatever you like," explains Sikes. He worked with Ken Linsteadt Architects and Denler Hobart Gardens to give the place a spirited remodel for a young family of four, all while respecting the original architecture. "[The clients] wanted something that was timeless," Sikes says, "but also happy and colorful and fun."

The first order of business was to turn what was originally two separate rooms for living and dining into one large gathering space. To balance this modernized layout, Sikes highlighted original details like millwork and trim with bold color pairings, most notably a rich coral wallpaper trimmed in sky blue. "We wanted to give it a bit of drama," the Los Angeles–based designer says. The thoughtful rearrangement also made room for additional storage: built-in cabinets on either side of the fireplace, and hutches for decorative and serving pieces. Downstairs is the kids' domain, with a TV and game room that opens up to the patio and pool—which also makes it ideal for entertaining.

"People want fresh air, and to be able to enjoy the outside as much as the inside," says Sikes, who has established himself as a go-to for homes with a kind of indoor-outdoor elegance. Outside, a variety of custom awnings diffuse just enough of the property's abundant sunshine. "It's really a place for a young family to share memories and energy and have fun," says Sikes. "And that's the best kind of house."
—

A blue-and-white palette in the living room channels the breezy feel of the rest of the home. *Sofa:* custom, in a Manuel Canovas fabric. *Coffee table:* Aesthetic Decor. *Bowl and candlesticks on table:* Rose Tarlow Melrose House.

(RIGHT) Sikes built in the cabinets flanking the fireplace, then lined them in the same fabric as the sofa across the room. *Table:* custom, Iatesta Studio. *Chairs:* Rigo's Custom Furniture, in Cowtan & Tout fabric. *Rug:* Vermilion. *Chandelier and floor lamp:* Circa Lighting. *Table lamp:* Paolo Mochino Ltd. *Mirror:* client's own.

"We wanted to give it a bit of drama."

PHILLIP THOMAS INC.
New York City

Behind the doors of a traditional Upper
East Side apartment is floor-to-ceiling eye candy.

Visitors to this Upper East Side apartment in New York City often do a double take. What at first glance looks like misty blue grass cloth on the walls of the living room is actually a meticulously custom-painted crosshatch pattern by Andrew Tedesco. "They wanted to amp it up!" says Phillip Thomas, the founder and principal designer of the New York–based firm Phillip Thomas Inc, of the unit in a classical pre-war building that he overhauled for former clients.

His agenda: Beef up the colors to super-saturated tones, mix and match sumptuous fabrics, and cloak every room in some kind of interesting wall treatment. Still, some surprises are highly practical: In the kitchen, what looks like silk wallpaper is really a very sneaky washable vinyl. Then there is the circus hiding in a powder room: "The husband is such a character, and that's technically his bathroom," Thomas laughs. "There's something about the paper that just reminds me of his joie de vivre; it captures his sophistication as well as his playfulness."

The designer first encountered the pattern—de Gournay Deco Monkeys—inside Loulou's, the exclusive nightclub in London where every room is papered in a different wild print. He never forgot it: "I mean, how can you help but smile when you walk in?"

Prints pop not only on the walls, but also on floorboards, sofas, pillows, and curtains. "It's a dialogue between all the different materials in a space," says Thomas. "Not everybody can be the leading lady. You have to have supporting actors and people behind the scenes."

At the end of the floor plan is a jewel box: the red-lacquered family room. "The higher the sheen, the less forgiving the surface will be," Thomas explains—but that didn't stop him from using it across every inch of wall and molding. The glossy gamble paid off. "The way light is reflected, the movement of light, it gives the space life," he explains. "It makes you really take note of the beauty."

—

The goal for the kitchen was "to create a space that was light and airy," says the designer. *Vinyl wallpaper:* Soie Végétale by Élitis. *Ceiling paint:* Mediterranean Breeze, Benjamin Moore. *Roman shade fabric:* Lanterns, Galbraith & Paul. *Chairs:* Serena & Lily.

(RIGHT) De Gournay Deco Monkeys wallpaper adds a playfulness to the powder room. "These clients are nothing if not colorful people—in the way they dress, the way they lead their lives, and their personalities," says Thomas.

LISA STONE DESIGN
Philadelphia

The work of Dutch painter Piet Mondrian inspired
the interiors of this art-filled home.

"Every project starts with a story, and this one was all about color," says designer Lisa Stone. For an apartment in a mid-century building in downtown Philadelphia's Rittenhouse Square, the work of Dutch painter Piet Mondrian was her muse. (The clients loved the colors red, blue, yellow, gray, white, and touches of black.) Then came the real work: "to reuse as much of the existing furniture as possible, good and bad," says Stone, "as [the clients] are both practical *and* sentimental."

Stone designed a sitting room with three spaces: one for card and game playing (a weekly ritual for the clients), one for TV watching, and one for casual friends and family gatherings. "The incredible view of Rittenhouse Square serves as a perfect backdrop for the spirited room," says the designer.

One unique component of the two-year project: Every single room features artwork by a notable artist, made possible by the clients' charitable efforts. In the early 1980s, they received a limited-edition portfolio of photographs and prints by Andy Warhol, Robert Rauschenberg, Richard Serra, Claes Oldenburg, and Peter Beard (to name a few), following a donation they made to celebrate the new home of the Anthology Film Archives, the first international center dedicated to the preservation and exhibition of avant-garde films and videos.

All the more fitting that the designer went with an artistic color scheme for the backdrop. Says the designer: "It's comfortable, classic, fresh, modern, and colorful, and has a joyful energy."

(PREVIOUS) "My clients' love of color and playfulness allowed for so much creative expression in the kitchen," says Stone. *Tile:* Quemere Designs. *Cabinetry:* custom, painted California Blue (lowers) and White Dove (uppers), both by Benjamin Moore. *Stools:* Jessica Charles. *Fabric:* Boussac Swing in Cerise, Pierre Frey. *Dining chairs:* Century Furniture in Pindler Meander in Lacquer.

86

A vintage sofa reupholstered in blue velvet by Kravet anchors a seating area designed for casual friend and family gatherings. *Coffee table and armchairs:* vintage, both in Schumacher fabric. *Chest of drawers:* Woodbridge Furniture. *Rug:* French Accents. *Lamps:* Circa Lighting with custom shades.

The go-to spot for weekly game nights: a custom card table covered in red grasscloth and surrounded by Vanguard chairs upholstered in Schumacher and Kerry Joyce fabrics. *Chandelier:* antique with custom shades. *Roman shade:* custom, in a Quadrille fabric.

(RIGHT) An iconic Hinson wallpaper pattern, "Fireworks," and the red-lacquer treatment on the bed in the guest room add a graphic hit that updates many of the clients' existing furniture pieces. *Bedding:* Serena & Lily. *Bolster and Roman shade:* custom, in a Schumacher fabric.

"It's comfortable, classic, fresh,
modern, and colorful, and has a joyful energy."

ARIENE BETHEA
Charlotte, North Carolina

Armed with a passed-down proclivity for collecting
cool stuff, one designer turned her home into a wonderland.

"I'm a collector first," says Ariene Bethea. That attitude is the foundation of her layered Charlotte, North Carolina, shop, Dressing Rooms Interiors Studio, which stocks an ever-evolving assortment of vintage and new home wares. But it also rings true in the colorful, art-filled home she shares with her husband (and dog). Bethea's methodology is simple: "I only buy things that I love, whether for my house or the store. It's not necessarily what's on trend at the time; if I love it, I'm gonna purchase it." The result is a delightfully eclectic mix—some of the motifs and styles Bethea gravitates toward are animals, crown molding, layered textures, and 1970s art.

While her current profession requires regular treasure hunting, Bethea's love of collecting dates back to childhood. Her parents and grandparents each had a discerning eye. At home, Bethea mixes her own finds with their family heirlooms: a 1960s Milo Baughman sofa (in its original upholstery!) that her mother purchased on layaway, a metal dining set of her grandparents' that Bethea revived with fabric remnants. Finding this mix comes naturally: "That's just how I grew up," she recalls. "We had masks, we had mid-century art, Asian art, African art, and abstract art, and it was all mixed together."

Setting the backdrop to Bethea's collection is an array of rich jewel tones, as well as detailed fixtures and molding—despite the home being a (now fifteen-year-old) new build. Her admiration for such ornate architectural details comes from the seven years she spent living in Boston, where she became enamored with historic New England homes. "I added that heavy molding wherever I could," she says. "Double molding, double crown—I fell in love with that style." In Bethea's hands, these traditional accents are anything but stuffy; instead, they provide a supporting framework for a perfectly personal home that, as Bethea says, "fits how we live and showcases the things that are important to us as a family."

(PREVIOUS) "It was pretty black-and-white at first and then I gradually started adding layers," Bethea says of the living room, which is grounded by a Robert Lawson painting that was her mother's. *Paint:* Smoke Grey, Glidden. *Carpet:* Surya. *Art:* Minted (over windows) and Texture Imports (seated figurine). *Curtains:* Martha & Ash, in Teresa Roche Art & Textiles fabric. *Coffee table:* Bernhardt. *Ottomans:* vintage.

"This bedroom was originally a really light blue," Bethea says. "But I realized after living in it that I didn't like waking up in a bright room." A hotel stay prompted the shift to a "moodier" hue, which Bethea found by mixing several Sherwin-Williams colors. *Art, mirror, mannequin, and sofa:* vintage. *Throw pillow:* MD Home Collection. *Bedspread:* Etsy. *Bolsters:* Swank Home Interiors. *Lamp:* Dressing Rooms Interiors Studio.

Bethea sourced the collection of masks from a fellow vintage dealer and displayed them in a riff on the gallery wall of her childhood home. *Table:* Caracole. *Chairs:* Universal Furniture. *Carpet:* Surya. *Sideboard:* Bernhardt.

(RIGHT) A Milo Baughman sofa from Bethea's mother finds new life in the lounge. *Paint:* Tricorn Black, Sherwin–Williams. *Mirror, sofa, elephant table, and lamps:* vintage. *Throw pillows:* custom, Jackie Rae Studios.

Red

(01)

Like biting into a very tart, crisp apple.

(02)

(03)

(04)

(05)

(01) This hand-painted Gracie wallpaper is a bold yet welcoming backdrop for warm wood accents in a dining room by Meredith McBrearty. *Chandelier:* Tuell + Reynolds. *Chairs:* Gregorius | Pineo. (02) Designer Birgitte Pearce used doors from a salvage auction to hide this pantry cabinet. *Paint:* Fine Paints of Europe Hollandlac satin enamel color-matched to NCS S 5040-R10B. (03) The use of cozy flokati rugs, a gingham Pindler fabric, and faux-bois stenciling on the walls of this bunk room by Amity Worrel was inspired by alpine cottages. *Millwork:* Domi Goods. *Sconces:* custom shades with brass wall mounts, D & W Lighting Showroom. (04) A famed Zebra print by Scalamandré is paired with vintage French sconces in a powder room by Starrett Hoyt Ringbom. (05) Designed by M. Lavender Interiors, this kids' playroom exudes cheery fun thanks to Benjamin Moore Strawberry Red on the walls.

(06)

(06) A pattern-rich mix of bold textiles gives this playroom by designer Kati Curtis a sense of worldly eclecticism. *Wall covering:* custom, Brett Design. *Drapery:* Christopher Farr Cloth. *Window seat:* Holland & Sherry fabric, with vintage and Jonathan Adler throw pillows. *Side table:* Herman Miller. *Chair and chandelier:* vintage. (07) Moorish and Mediterranean touches influenced this patio by Sheldon Harte. *Furniture:* Michael Taylor Designs, in Link outdoor fabric. *Table:* Formations. *Terra-cotta tiles:* Concept Studio. (08) Playful red bed frames enliven an Erin Sander design. *Wallpaper:* Lulie Wallace.

(07)

(08)

5 DESIGNER-APPROVED
Red Paints

—

"When I incorporate reds, I tend to go more with a deep wine tone to give it depth and maturity. Self-Portrait by Backdrop makes you feel as if you fell into a large glass of Malbec."

—

TYSON NESS,
principal of *Studio Ness*

"Bright and bold colors, like Russet Rust by Asian Paints, have a unique ability to look mellow in sunlight and dramatic in the evening glow."

—

KRSNAA MEHTA,
principal of *India Circus*

"Pinks and reds to me are synonymous with frozen drinks and relaxing. Benjamin Moore Chili Pepper is a really deep coral."

—

RICHARD MISHAAN,
principal of *Richard Mishaan Design*

"A deep, cozy red, Stolen Kiss by Sherwin-Williams is timeless and inviting, with a lovely sense of warmth."

—

SANDRA LUCAS,
principal of *Lucas/Eilers Design Associates*

"Warm and inviting, Rookwood Red by Sherwin-Williams is suitable for areas where there is not much natural light, as it casts its own glow."

—

COURTNEY MCLEOD,
principal of *Right Meets Left Interior Design*

(11)

(12)

(09) Walls upholstered in Home Couture fabric lend a sophisticated edge to Mally Skok's traditional dining room. (10) Hand-stenciled faux bois walls by Julia Rogers in this Amity Worrel–designed home "add character and richness" paired with red accents. (11) A vibrant red transforms traditional built-in shelving in an office by Mary-Bryan Peyer. (12) A red quilt paired with the classic Sister Parish fabric Kismet dials up the nostalgia in this kid's room by Cameron Ruppert. *Wallpaper: Cath Kidston.*

(13)

(13) Checkerboard linoleum and lobster-red details give antique items new life in the laid-back kitchen of designer Tom Scheerer. *Wallpaper:* Tom Scheerer for Quadrille.

LIVE COLORFULLY

Pale Pastels

Like the DUSTY BLUES and BLUSH PINKS of dawn, wispy colors can lift even the lowest spirits. Soft and undeniably pretty, these watercolor interiors are the visual equivalent of hitting refresh.

BARRY DIXON
Washington, D.C.

Contents: two adults, four kids, a dog, and some incredible decor.

(PREVIOUS) In the living room, the Cochin Shell pink by C2 Paint acts as a neutral, uniting eclectic furnishings and accessories without overwhelming the space. *Table:* Julian Chichester.

A sitting area is soothing in all blues. *Paint:* Well Water, C2 Paint. *Sconces:* Arteriors. *Chandelier:* Crowder Designs. *Club chairs:* Zentique.

"Find wonderful things that you love, and no matter where you move, they'll find their place."

"It's an elusive color," says Virginia-based designer Barry Dixon of the blush walls on the living room of this Washington, D.C., house. "A pale terra-cotta or a faded brick color, a pale clay. Everyone looks beautiful in that room." The color, Cochin Shell, isn't a vestige of the 1970s, from when the house was built; Dixon created it for his line at C2 Paint, and it's matched exactly to the pigment of an egg laid by a heritage-breed hen on his farm in Virginia.

A room awash in rosé might be a leap for some clients, but the designer had a pretty good hunch this client would go for it. Dixon first worked with the family years ago, when they had one toddler son and another son on the way. Two things have changed since then: The family gained a third son, and, finally, a daughter. Enter a very pink bedroom that is magically unlike the pink living room, due to a cooler undertone (along with heart pillows and an abundance of stuffed animals). "It's a girlier pink, sort of frothier," he says, "a color we call Belle's Nose," which is another of his C2 paints. "Belle is one of my goats at the barn, and her nose is exactly that shade of pink."

Color is often a jumping-off point for Dixon. "I wouldn't use blues in, say, a dining room, because it's not really a color that stimulates appetite," he says. "As I go up in a house, skyward, we use more blues. I'll put blue in a bedroom simply because it is a serene color to fall asleep in." Indeed, a soothing cornflower appears in the primary bedroom, a color called Well Water, while one son's room is in Approaching Storm, both by C2.

While the kids' rooms reflect their current personalities (another son's room is a smoky amethyst color, inspired by his rock collection), they are built to last. "I think the shell and the base of furnishings should grow with them. You can replace the daughter's little heart pillows with more serious pillows as she gets older," Dixon says. Already, the design has proved its longevity: The artwork, ottoman, and drapes in the daughter's room were all used in the family's previous formal living room.

"It really is about the mix," he says. "If you mix old with new, mid-century modern with Colonial, futuristic chrome tables with old French chairs, you hit a point where everything is timeless."

"You know the magnolia pods that are left when big blossoms fall away?" Dixon muses. That's what inspired this pendant he designed for Avrett. *Curtains:* Barry Dixon for Vervain. *Chests:* Dessin Fournir. *Chairs:* Ironies, in an Osborne & Little fabric.

(RIGHT) In the daughter's room, a jib door feels like a secret passageway. *Art:* Feathers by Paule Marrot. *Ottoman:* in a shagreen vinyl by Celerie Kemble. *Pendant:* Arteriors.

LIVE COLORFULLY

CAROLINE RAFFERTY INTERIORS
Palm Beach, Florida

To create this beachy oasis,
one designer simply looked to the world around her.

Rattan, jute, and a pile of seashells. Going all out with tropical materials can put you at risk of becoming a boho-chic cliché. So when Caroline Rafferty, a Palm Beach designer known for creating mod, Euro-tinged interiors, was tasked with creating a Bahamian style getaway down the road, she knew she'd have to put her own spin on it.

"Usually if someone wants that look, I'm not the first person they'd call!" she laughs. But homeowner Melanie Charlton Fowler, founder of luxury closet company Clos-ette, was a longtime friend, and Rafferty knew she had great taste. "She came to me with a vision," says the designer. "She and her husband loved Tom Scheerer's work in Lyford Cay, so I made it my job to guide her to her own version of that."

One of Charlton's ideas was a shell-covered fireplace. "It definitely could have gone in a very different direction and become kitschy," Rafferty admits. "So instead of using big conch shells, we used a single layer of smaller shells so that it would feel like a mosaic. It's a real piece of art." And when Fowler mentioned an old-school sea-grape wall mural at her local tennis club, Rafferty enlisted her decorative painter to create an updated version for the home. "We tried to interpret it in a new way, making the design more open and changing the colors," she says.

For the palette, Rafferty used pinks, pistachio greens, and ocean-hued blues both indoors and out—albeit carefully. "It can easily go saccharine when you bunch pastels together," she says, "so I was always thinking about ways to keep it fresh, whether it was by adding materials like metal, stone, and natural fibers, or mixing in other colors, like black."

The final result captures both Fowler's island-inspired vision and Rafferty's eclecticism. "If anyone else had come to me and said, 'I want a copy of a Bahamian home,' I probably wouldn't have thought I could do it," says Rafferty. "But by taking all the best elements of the style and mixing them up, we made it original!"

—

To break up the long, narrow room, Rafferty created a pair of conversation nooks anchored by Lee Industries sofas in a Sunbrella fabric (Sailor by Lulu DK for Duralee). *Art:* Henri Maik (left) and Simeon Braguin (right). *Wall mural:* Joseph Steiert. *Side tables:* Frontgate (blue); Currey & Company (hourglass). *Wicker lamps:* Celerie Kemble for Arteriors. *Rugs:* Madeline Weinrib.

JANIE MOLSTER DESIGNS
Richmond, Virginia

Each room of this family home functions as its own little getaway.

"When they're home, they really want to be at home," says Richmond-based interior designer Janie Molster of her clients, Ammar and Sara Sarraf, two full-time doctors with three young kids. "They're so committed to their careers, and they also have this busy growing family that, you know, needs full attention." The couple called on Molster to help them turn an outdated 1950s cottage in a leafy Richmond neighborhood into a fully functional family retreat. "They did have a long wish list," Molster recalls. "They wanted to be able to spread out."

This meant the house would need to be renovated "down to the studs," per Molster, then expanded to include a more comfortably sized kitchen and dining room, plus larger living spaces and bedrooms. "We almost doubled the square footage," Sara says. And the light: The new dining room has a 14-foot cathedral ceiling. But it's the details in each room that reflect the family's passion for getting out and seeing the world.

"When we first got married, we went to a ton of different places, and later with the kids," Sara says. "And I've just always loved the Mediterranean." A collection of imports—Italian Savonarola dining chairs, multiple Moroccan rugs—are mixed with American-made pieces: ombré curtains in Kevin O'Brien Studio velvet, a Hubbardton Forge chandelier, works by Southern artists. In the son's room, Molster covered the angled ceiling above the bed in a blown-up world map to inspire dreams of the family's next destination: "Kids need a retreat just like we need a retreat," she says. "You want to have this sort of romantic feeling of being transported elsewhere, because with young children, it's often hard to be anywhere else."

(LEFT) From the wood vessels on the shelves to the fireplace brick and the shaggy rug, a variety of textures lend nuance to the earthy palette. *Bench:* Highland House. *Chair:* Oggetti. *Armchairs:* Lee Industries. *Rug:* custom, Janie Molster Designs. *Artwork:* vintage.

(ABOVE) Curtains in ombré Kevin O'Brien Studio fabric give the primary bedroom a luxurious feel. *Paint:* Adagio, Benjamin Moore. *Pendant:* Fortuny. *Wallpaper:* Cowtan & Tout. *Desk:* Bungalow 5. *Chair:* Global Views. *Bed and bedding:* Modern History. *Rug:* Rosecore.

LIVE COLORFULLY

SHERRELL DESIGN STUDIO
Houston

How one designer cleverly disguised
awkward angles to create an elegant space.

(PREVIOUS) Neal found this bench for under $100 at a local antiques store, then stripped, gesso-finished, and upholstered it in a bold purple. "It makes it a little fresh, a little new, and kind of mixes that traditional with a little bit more of a contemporary feel," she explains. *Art:* Wendover Art Group.

(RIGHT) "I love a stripe," says Neal. *Headboard:* custom, through Sherrell Design Studio with Samuel & Sons trim. *Pillow:* custom, through Sherrell Design Studio, in Kravet fabric. *Bolster:* custom, through Sherrell Design Studio, using Pindler fabric, Samuel & Sons trim, and Schumacher cording. *Desk:* Ann Gish, Global Views. *Lamp:* Circa Lighting. *Paint:* Chantilly Lace, Benjamin Moore.

(FOLLOWING LEFT) A chandelier by Julie Neill provided a jumping-off point for the whole room. "I just loved how abstract it is, and the feel of the plaster," the designer says. *Wallpaper:* Lulu and Georgia. *Art:* Wendover Art Group. *Chairs:* Schumacher.

(FOLLOWING RIGHT) The television is hidden behind a large Paule Marrot print from Natural Curiosities. *Sofa:* custom, Lee Jofa, in Suzanne Kasler fabric. *Light fixture:* custom.

When Houston designer Sherrell Neal first set eyes on the 1997 house she and her husband would call home, the designer knew that "it needed a lot of updating." Besides some ornate, "very old-school Texas" wallpapering in unlikely places like the bathroom, the biggest issue was the awkward layout. "There were a lot of weird angles and nightmare corners; there's nearly no storage." But the couple was unfazed. "Being in the design industry, we could see a lot of potential," she says.

Without undertaking a complete gut renovation, Neal set out to turn a wonky layout with outdated design choices into a layered, welcoming home. As a first step, she established a soothing off-white color palette supplemented with lavender, wisteria, and icy blue to soften some of the geometry. "I love color and I love pattern but I can definitely live in a tone-on-tone space," says Neal. "I think there's something so calming and kind of romantic about it." That was the credo in the primary bedroom, which envelops its inhabitants with soft textures. "I really just wanted this space to bring our blood pressure down," says Neal. "We are busy people, so just to have a sanctuary of our own was what really drove the color palette for this space."

Yet there are also moments of boldness. "I wanted to offset a lot of the softness in the living room with something really strong and abstract," Neale says. The subtlety in the rest of the room is pulled from the color story in the entry painting, with a custom sofa upholstered in a beige Suzanne Kasler stripe from Lee Jofa and swivel chairs covered in a light blue. In the guest room, Brunschwig & Fils' Talavera wallpaper "was the perfect jumping-off point," she says. "It has this shiny reflection when the light hits it." The result is a home that feels like a cloud—and looks entirely of-the-moment.

ARIEL OKIN INTERIORS
Westchester County, New York

Smart splurges and lots of layers in a
once-bland home create an instant lived-in look.

LIVE COLORFULLY

"Pale blues and greens are my favorite colors, which I wove throughout the rooms for a cohesive color story and a relaxing effect," Okin says of the mix in the living room. *Sofa:* Society Social. *Chair:* Kenian. *Rugs:* Cailini Coastal (large blue); Chairish (small green and blue kilim). *Lamp:* Hudson Valley Lighting. *Coffee table:* Ariel Okin for Society Social. *Side table:* vintage, Kittinger. *Window treatments:* The Shade Store.

Ariel Okin didn't plan on moving to the suburbs. But after she, her husband, and their young daughter showed up at her husband's parents' home as COVID-19 was sweeping New York City, they found they loved it there so much they wanted to stay. A year and a half later, Okin created the family home of her dreams in Westchester County, New York, from a simple blank slate—emphasis on *blank*.

"Our house had been rented out for about seven years when we bought it, so the owners were not keen on doing much to it design-wise except maintenance," explains the designer. "It had a dated beige kitchen and a lot of beige wallpaper; it also had some dark red toile wallpaper in the dining room, so my main goal was to lighten it up and make it feel really cozy and lived in, like we'd been here for a few years."

But she also felt that the neutral base would allow a playful blend of colors and accessories while still feeling serene. "I wanted the house to feel clean and edited but layered and cheerful," Okin says. With the good bones of the structure intact, her task became peeling back the outdated additions of the last fifteen years and replacing them with a mix of classic textile patterns, soft colors, and natural textures.

"I think English country homes are unabashed with their color combinations in a really confident, unstudied way," Okin says. "The English aren't afraid to take risks with a riot of colors, which I find really inspiring." She followed their lead by peppering pale blues and greens around the house "to create a cohesive color story and a relaxing effect." For a dash of the unexpected, Okin went with Farrow & Ball Breakfast Room Green on the millwork and trim in the mudroom and incorporated pops of yellow in the lampshades in the formal living room. "They felt a bit off key—in a good way," she explains.

Other rooms echo a more modern approach. "I tried to mix those colors with contemporary artwork and clean furniture silhouettes for an updated take that feels fresh and appropriate for a young family," says Okin, as the Saarinen table in the breakfast nook suggests. "But I'm also a magpie and hoard vintage textiles, so there's always something new draped over a sofa, whether it's a vintage suzani with embroidered pomegranates tossed over a sectional or a random pink throw I found." Lived-in it certainly is.

—

"Our biggest splurge was painting and wallpapering the house, but it really made such a difference," Okin says. "It honestly turned the house into a completely new space." *Wallcovering: Ariel Okin for The Mural Source. Rug: Caroline Gidiere for King's House. Sideboard, table, and dining chairs (the latter in Fabricut velvet): antique.*

(RIGHT) For an outdoor sitting area, Okin "really wanted both space to lounge, and space to have dinner and entertain, so I created separate zones," the designer explains. *Furniture, pillows, and rug: Serena & Lily.*

LIVE COLORFULLY

PHOEBE HOWARD
Palm Beach, Florida

Turns out you *can* teach an old house new tricks.

(PREVIOUS) Newly vaulted ceilings prevent the space from feeling cramped. "Still, we kept all the furniture low-slung," Howard says. *Shades:* Joss Graham. *Rug:* Brukvin.

(RIGHT) In the wet bar, swiveling vintage barstools have seats embroidered with a duck in a nest that the client's daughter designed, a nod to the home's longtime nickname. *Paint:* Palisades Park, Benjamin Moore. *Bar:* custom, Leeds. *Pendant:* vintage, Mario Lopez Torres. *Sconces:* Soane Britain. *Flooring:* custom, painted by Seabreeze Building.

"It transports you back in time somehow."

Cats are notoriously picky—it's part of their personal brand. So when designer Phoebe Howard flung open the doors of this 1891 Victorian to find countless feral felines, she took it as a good omen. The home's scalloped shingles and ornate gabled roofs had cast a spell over the neighbors, Julie and Brian Simmons, who then hired Howard to save the building—by turning it into their guesthouse.

The cats were the least of it. "The Duck's Nest," as the second-oldest house in Palm Beach is called, "just had become so run-down—but it's protected by the Historical Society, so you weren't allowed to tear it down and start over," says Howard. Years of termite and water damage had torn through the structure, and the existing foundation was hair-raising: made of stacked bricks and a 25-foot-wide tree stump. But with the help of two architects, Meghan Ford Taylor of Seabreeze Building and Roger Janssen of Dailey Janssen Architects, Howard persevered and was able to revamp the place to make it suitable for a new generation.

"We knew we wanted it to feel old and cranky, but not be falling-down cranky, so it's filled with a lot of vintage furniture," says Howard, who sourced nearly every item in the house secondhand. Low ceilings were vaulted and outfitted with caned paneling, and an old screened porch was converted to a more functional, but no less restorative, air-conditioned sunroom.

The home's original stained-glass windows inspired a retro, candy-color palette that suits the old soul of the home. "This is kind of the opposite of a peaceful, calm space. But it does, at the same time, transport you somewhere— back in time somehow," says Howard. "It just makes you feel good when you go in there."

136

For the screened porch–turned–sunroom, Howard selected a U-shaped, 12-foot-long armless number with white cotton brush fringe from MSDC, affectionately calling it "the Big Green Monster." *Paint:* Horizon, Benjamin Moore. *Coffee table and boat charts:* vintage. *Pendant:* Soane Britain. *Pillows:* Mrs. Howard. *Chairs:* vintage, in Peter Dunham fabric. *Wood table:* A. Tyner Antiques. *Flooring:* Villa Lagoon Tile.

THE 50% *Trick*

—

Don't limit yourself to the standard colors you find in hardware store paint decks. To achieve a custom look with very little effort (and budget), designers rely on this simple yet genius secret: the fractional blend. "Lightening a paint can create a whole new shade," says Howard. "I take the color that I thought I wanted and cut it to 75%, 50%, and 25% strength with Benjamin Moore Super White. Often it looks like a completely different color."

139

Pink

(Mood Board)

(01)

Rooms with an inherently rosy disposition.

(01) Nicole Dohmen of Atelier ND Interior worked with several paint brands to customize colors for the home of actor Carice van Houten. *Window treatments:* Helene Blanche (Roman shades); Étoffe (curtains). *Table:* Sabine Marcelis. *Dining chairs:* vintage Afra and Tobia Scarpa for Gavina, in Pierre Frey mohair. (02) Inspired by a photo of London veiled in cherry blossoms, this formal living room by designer Bruce Fox is at once elegant and approachable. *Paint:* Pink Ground, Farrow & Ball. *Art:* William McLure. *Sofa:* custom, McLaughlin Upholstery, in de Le Cuona fabric. (03) The blush walls of this living room by Lilse McKenna act as a neutral. *Paint:* Pink Ground, Farrow & Ball. *Sofa:* custom, in Gainsborough Velvet with pillows in Brighton Pavilion, both Schumacher. *Lamp:* Bunny Williams Home with Perrotine shade. (04) A graceful shade of pink, El Mirage by Portola Paints & Glazes, balances out a plaid runner in a stairway by Elspeth Benoit and A1000X Better.

5 DESIGNER-APPROVED
Pink Paints
—

"Farrow & Ball Dead Salmon has a versatility and sophistication unrivaled in other, similar hues."

—

ZOË FELDMAN, principal of *Zoë Feldman Design*

"The earthiness of Potter's Clay lime wash by Portola Paints & Glazes keeps the citrus-based pink from being juvenile or overly feminine."

—

VIRGINIA TOLEDO, principal of *Toledo Geller*

"We recently chose Rose Ottoman by Ressource Peintures in a plaster finish for a peaceful and calming effect in a primary bedroom."

—

JESSICA WILPON KAMEL, principal of *Ronen Lev*

"Sherwin-Williams Diminutive Pink works wonders on ceilings and casts the most beautiful light on your face at dinner parties."

—

COURTNAY TARTT ELIAS, principal of *Creative Tonic Design*

"A pale blush color, Pink Ground by Farrow & Ball gives a room an all-over, soft, even, warm glow—thus creating a calming and comforting environment."

—

JONATHAN BERGER, principal of *Jonathan Berger Interior Design Associates*

(05)

(06)

(07)

(05) Farrow & Ball Rangwali gives gray cabinetry an edge in a kitchen by Alicia Hassnen of Brooklinteriors. (06) A whimsical canopied daybed doubles as a reading nook in *Country Living* editor in chief Rachel Hardage Barrett's daughter's room, designed with Heather Chadduck Hillegas. Canopy fabric: John Robshaw. *Skirt fabric:* Quadrille. (07) In her own den, designer Janie Molster paired pink walls (Confetti by Benjamin Moore) with a fanciful Sunbrella stripe on an antique sofa.

(08)

(08) To keep this pink bedroom from feeling childish, designer Sasha Bikoff went with a sophisticated tonal approach.
Wallpaper: Rubelli. Lamp: Fortuny. Bed: vintage, upholstered in Fendi fabric.

(10)

(11)

(09) Textile designer Krsnaa Mehta embraced a more-is-more aesthetic in the study of his apartment, using both pink and purple walls as the backdrop for a collection of artwork. Shade, table, and chair: BARO Design. (10) Circadian-rhythm color lights turn this cream bathroom by HGTV personality Breegan Jane temporarily pink. Vanity light and mirror: RH. Counter and kick: Golden Lightning marble from Rock Mill Tile & Stone. (11) A pastel hue—Farrow & Ball Middleton Pink—on the walls tempers bright bursts of fuchsia and green in a bedroom by Cecilia Casagrande. Ceiling light: Alexa Hampton for Circa Lighting. Art above fireplace: Christopher Peter.

LIVE COLORFULLY

Warm Neutrals

CREAM, FLAX, CHARCOAL, CHOCOLATE—
some of the most comforting colors are pulled from the natural
world, creating calming respites from all the noise of daily life.

LIVE COLORFULLY

M. ELLE DESIGN
Deer Valley, Utah

Spread across a series of cabins, this family
compound is designed to host multiple generations at once.

Procuring the trunks for the boys' room proved quite the scavenger hunt: "The client had this one trunk and she really wanted to use it, but we had to find ones that kind of matched, or were similar," Carson recalls. "We scoured the Internet until we found the right ones." A worthwhile hunt for the perfect touch. *Beds:* RH. *Rug:* Contempo Floor Coverings. *Pendant:* Original BTC.

"They wanted it to be like a family camp." Sisters Marie Turner Carson and Emily Turner Barker, co-founders of California-based M. Elle Design, took this directive from a Utah client very literally. Tucked into the mountains at Victory Ranch, a development just outside Deer Valley, the spread belonged to an active, close-knit family who wasn't interested in the kitschy rough wood aesthetic of so many homes in the area. Working with Bob White of Forest Studio, the design team came up with an ultra-luxurious scheme that married community with a deep appreciation for nature.

To start, they conceived an untraditional layout in which, Carson says, "the guest rooms are like their own little cabins"—the perfect setup for a multigenerational family that loves to host. "We wanted to get away from the idea of the traditional lodge style, where it's a bunch of rooms in a big box, and instead break that down into this compound idea, where there are buildings that are moving along the river and the geometry is changing," says White, who worked with the late local builder Ivan Broman on the project.

Structures are built into the rolling landscape and arranged around connecting courtyards. By optimizing the property's incredible vistas, this layout offers guests a continual sense of discovery as they move between cabins. "All of the major rooms have these perfectly framed views," says White, who did all of his space planning on-site and imagined the new build as if it were a historic home gradually shaped over time. "I used that concept of a homestead added to over generations to bring a sense of authenticity," he says.

The structure is the ideal backdrop for the clients who, Carson says, "just really wanted to be with their family and their friends—and wanted everyone to feel at home and have their own place."

(PREVIOUS) The home's most open space, the living room is centered around a monumental fireplace. Carson layered in wool rugs and textural throws and pillows on the furniture, which is arranged in two sections to better accommodate multiple guests. *Sofa:* custom, M. Elle Design, in Loro Piana and Kneedler Fauchère fabrics. *Chairs:* AM Designs. *Chandelier:* custom, Hélène Aumont. *Ottoman:* custom, M. Elle Design.

(ABOVE) For the youngest generation of visitors, Carson conceived a tasteful take on camp bunks, with a room of rush beds for the girls. "We really wanted this part to feel like summer camp, but we didn't want it to feel like the exact same bed over and over so we changed it with different bedding or different decorative pillows," Carson says. *Beds:* Noir Furniture LA. *Bedding:* Chelsea Textiles. *Chandeliers:* Paul Ferrante.

"All of the major rooms
have these perfectly framed views."

LIVE COLORFULLY

Fortuny velvet lends depth to the rustic neutral backdrop of this cozy seating arrangement. *Coffee table:* Sawkille Co. *Sconce:* Dessin Fournir. *Side tables:* Rose Uniacke. *Rug:* Mitchell Denburg Collection.

The dramatic, dark space is set on what is essentially a bridge, a cantilevered hallway connecting various rooms of the house. *Table:* custom, M. Elle Design with Bespoke Furniture. *Guest chairs:* AM Designs, in Loro Piana and Colefax and Fowler fabrics. *Host chairs:* custom, M. Elle Design with Bespoke Furniture, in Holland & Sherry fabric. *Pendant:* BK Antiques.

SEAN ANDERSON DESIGN
Memphis, Tennessee

A Tudor home gets a cozy, refined look thanks to countless vintage accents.

"That's part of our Southern culture and heritage: to embrace the imperfections in things."

A home doesn't need a major remodel to feel revived. Thoughtful rearranging and a few fresh pieces can do wonders, as the Memphis-based interior designer Sean Anderson illustrated in the home he redecorated for his former partner. What was once a house with a country vibe is now a sophisticated space brimming with antiques.

Built in the early 1990s, the modern-leaning Tudor has been an ongoing project for the homeowner, who bought the four-bedroom, four-bathroom residence with the intention of making it his forever home. Over the past several years, he has collected antiques for the house, but he wanted a refresh before embarking on major renovations, so he enlisted Anderson, who once lived there, to breathe in new life. "Since we have this history and he trusts me, he really gave me full rein to interpret the house the way I saw fit," Anderson says.

Over six days, Anderson and his team emptied the entire home and reintroduced all of the furniture and decor into new rooms. Most of the home features previously loved items from sources such as 1stDibs, Etsy, and local antique markets. Anderson also pulled from the client's attic full of antiques, as well as from the designer's existing on-display collection and his own firm's warehouse, where he had been setting aside pieces with the client in mind.

While each room flowed well and was beautiful prior to the redecoration, not every room was used. "Now, the homeowner can go to every space on a daily basis," Anderson says. "And he does—every part of this house is utilized."

"That's part of our Southern culture and heritage: to embrace the imperfections in things. We use what some people see as scrap or junk and show it in a refined way."

(OPENER) Here, "like everywhere else in the house, I was faced with having to work with underwhelming architectural details," Anderson says. "I used this opportunity to layer and fill the space with items that told the story of the client." *Paint:* Classic Gray, Benjamin Moore. *Art:* Buddy Whitlock. *Sofa:* RH. *Table:* antique from La Maison. *Rug:* Etsy.

(PREVIOUS) Anderson repurposed some beautiful panels, which the homeowner had kept for years in his attic, as a headboard. *Lighting:* antique from Revival Home. *Bench:* antique from Architectural Heritage. *Rug:* Etsy. *Bedding:* custom, Great Plains for Holly Hunt via Jim Thompson.

(LEFT) "I opted to lighten things up but still keep things warm and organic," the designer says of the inverted color scheme in a second bedroom. *All furnishings:* vintage.

159

(LEFT) "We wanted to use this space as a comfortable setting to observe some of these treasures while enjoying morning coffee," Anderson says. Standout pieces include the framed collection of arrows accumulated over years of antique shopping. *Paint:* Iron Ore, Sherwin-Williams. *Curtains:* RH. *Chandelier:* Chapman & Myers for Circa Lighting. *Tables and rug:* antique. *Sofa:* client's own.

(ABOVE) Wood accents temper the moody atmosphere—courtesy of walls and a ceiling clad in Iron Ore by Sherwin-Williams—in this masculine guest room.

1 PAINT, *Four Lights*

—

How SHERWIN-WILLIAMS Iron Ore reads in four different parts of this home.

LIVE COLORFULLY

AMBER EL-AMIN
Sterling, Virginia

A Moroccan rug dealer's eclectic home is a vintage-lover's dream.

When your job takes you to some of the world's most evocative destinations, it's only natural to channel them in your own home—even if that home is a 1990s-era house in Sterling, Virginia. "I believe the best design elements are full of soul and capable of expanding your experiences," says Amber El-Amin, who sells rugs through her online shop, The Gardener's House, and has made a habit of picking up homewares on her travels. "I went down to Marrakech and risked all of my savings on these twelve amazing collector rugs. I had never seen anything like them before," she recalls of the trip that inspired her to open an Etsy shop—and then design her home as a place to showcase her newfound passion.

Though the house is definitely of a time, she was drawn to its "good bones," and liked the worldly feel of the extra-high ceilings and interior balcony; she knew they would make a good backdrop for her eclectic finds, many of which were purchased at flea markets, online, and in back-alley antiques stores. Persistence was key. "I have in mind what I want and I keep looking," she says. Among her prized possessions are a 1940s Tiffany Studios–style shell lamp in the bedroom, a 1980s Milo Baughman–style credenza in the office, and a Paolo Buffa wood-frame sofa that would now be a fortune on 1stDibs. "Nearly everything in my house is vintage," says El-Amin, who has stories for every piece in every room and credits nature and history as the best designers.

The tonal living room feels upscale yet laid back, thanks to the menagerie of plants in Japanese and Algerian Berber Kabyle pottery. The sofa, a 1970s piece, was taken from a Palm Springs mansion, while the nineteenth-century Victorian marble fireplace mantel was purchased from a Boston bank executive's office. The plastered fireplace was renovated to feel more European. "I wanted something different that had some meaningful detail to it," says El-Amin. "The shape is actually inspired by the casbah in Tangier."

Through the years, El-Amin, who is half Moroccan and half German, has lived in India, Turkey, London, and Bologna, Italy, where she worked as an au pair before ultimately coming back to her Moroccan roots. This house may not be her forever home, but it certainly has the look of one that will stand the test of time. —

(PREVIOUS) A menagerie of plants in Japanese and Algerian Berber Kabyle pottery pepper the space. *Armchairs:* attributed to Fritz Hansen, from the 1940s. *Italian marble coffee table:* similar by Mario Bellini. *Sconce:* René Mathieu.

(RIGHT) A Milo Baughman–style Henredon credenza from the 1970s is one of El-Amin's prized posessions. *Coffee table:* calacatta viola marble. *Art:* Eduardo Chillida lithograph. *Rug:* 1960s Moroccan.

(PREVIOUS LEFT) An Urban Outfitters bed frame looks right at home amid all the vintage pieces.

(PREVIOUS RIGHT) El-Amin says persistence is the key to antique shopping. "I have in mind what I want and I keep looking."

(LEFT) The sofa, a 1970s piece taken from a Palm Springs mansion, once measured 22 feet (as it was part of a sectional!), while the nineteenth-century Victorian marble fireplace mantel was purchased from a Boston bank executive's office. *Armchairs:* attributed to Fritz Hansen, from the 1940s. *Italian marble coffee table:* similar by Mario Bellini.

169

JAE JOO DESIGNS
Boston

A soft palette (and a sledgehammer)
brings an unloved 1885 rowhouse to modern glory.

LIVE COLORFULLY

The vintage Jindřich Halabala designs (in BDDW fabric) are "good newspaper-reading chairs," says Joo. *Table:* custom, Jerry Nance. *Lamp:* Chapman & Myers. *Curtain fabric:* Rogers & Goffigon. *Pillow fabric:* Rosemary Hallgarten. *Rug:* J. Namnoun Rug Gallery.

"Everything feels sort of candlelit," says designer Jae Joo of the home in Boston's Back Bay neighborhood that she gut renovated over the course of three years. "I didn't want the home to feel too bright or too crisp, so I purposely picked colors that are on the warmer side." Joo knew the client wasn't a "bright-light person" from spending time in her previous homes—it was her mother-in-law.

For her husband's parents, Colleen and Ed, Joo faced a paradox: How do you tear apart an 1885 rowhouse and rebuild it such that it looks untouched? The New York–based designer satisfied both desires by choosing timeless new furnishings and materials while maintaining the best of the old stuff. "If we found any architectural detail intact that was known to be historic, we kept and restored it," Joo says. To wit: the kitchen. "When we first did a walk-through of the house, I remember being mesmerized by the original butler's pantry cabinetry." The team carefully removed it from the brick walls, rehabbed the boxes down to the hardware, and installed it back in the main kitchen. The original glass fronts survived the whole process.

From there, Joo layered in antiques from 1stDibs and memorabilia from her in-laws' travels. ("They're all vintage and real and all from the garage," she says.) And she carved out space for their hobbies—pairs of chairs for reading, a deep window seat so their grandkids can watch the Red Sox while they cook, and a hidden sound system connecting the rooms. Visible electronics would have been contrary to the vibe.

So were her clients pleased, or was Joo in for an awkward holiday season? Says Colleen, "When we first moved in, the music was turned on and Ed and I danced in each room— and around all the contractors."

173

1 PAINT,
Four Lights

—

How FARROW & BALL
Cromarty reads in four
different parts of this home.

(ABOVE) For a "refined yet
grand entrance," the designer
chose Gracie wallpaper. *Sconces:*
Circa Lighting. *Mirror:* Made Goods.
Table: Soane Britain. *Umbrella
holder:* vintage leather.

(RIGHT) At the beginning of
the design process, Joo brought
her mother-in-law, Colleen, to
the BDDW showroom, where they
bought the table, console, and
plates. *Chairs and bench:* Pierre
Jeanneret-inspired. *Chandelier:*
Apparatus. *Shades:* Élitis Fabrics.
The design team painstakingly
removed layers of old paint to
reveal the original brick.

LIVE COLORFULLY

KRYSTAL MATTHEWS DESIGN
Baton Rouge, Louisiana

A nineteenth-century farmhouse
moves to new digs—but stays true to its old soul.

(PREVIOUS) Where the farmhouse required new flooring, Matthews laid down 8-inch pine and stained it two colors (Provincial and Dark Walnut by Minwax) to match the original boards. *Paint:* Pure White, Sherwin-Williams. *Pendant:* Design Public. *Art:* Jennifer Lewis. *Table:* bought at auction from a Louisiana State University library. *Chairs:* vintage. *Console:* Hooker Furniture.

(LEFT) Centrally located in the house, the kitchen "had to create a soft flow to all the spaces while maintaining a voice of its own," says Matthews. *Tiles:* Equipe. *Sconces:* Thomas O'Brien for Circa Lighting. *Range:* Bertazzoni.

(RIGHT) Sourced from a hodgepodge of estate sales and street vendors, her art collection extends up onto the ceiling. *Pendant:* Wayfair. *Bedding:* Kate Spade (sheets), IKEA (shams), Etsy (bolster). *Table lamp:* Ralph Lauren Home. *Rug:* Rugs USA.

It was practically begging to be moved: The former owner of this 3,600-square-foot farmhouse knew the home was in the wrong place—so they literally had it cut into three pieces, loaded onto a trailer, and driven to a woodsy country-club community near Baton Rouge, Louisiana. And that's exactly where Krystal Matthews fell in love with it, while hunting for a place her family of five could really put down some roots. "It just has this charm, everyone who comes in feels it," she says of the 130-year-old structure. Given that Krystal and her husband, Blake Matthews, flip houses for a living, they were able to transform the old home to suit their needs at warp speed, buying in April 2020 and moving in by midsummer.

Imagining what the house would have felt like in its heyday, the Matthewses gave it a fresh—but contextualized—look. "We peeled away previous renovations, stripping it down to its original cedar walls, while keeping an eye on its historic Southern architecture," Krystal says. A few fresh coats of paint—Aesthetic White and Urbane Bronze by Sherwin-Williams—give the old farmhouse exterior a modern feel. The raised-floor construction, "adapted from Portugal, the West Indies, Africa, and Haiti, and great for air circulation in our muggy climate," was preserved, as were several alcoves that sold the designer from the start. "Each kid—Isabella, Ava-Claire, and Charles—has two window nooks in their bedroom, and their bathrooms do, too," she says. Onto these bones were added new flooring, picture molding, and mantels, all in homage to the home's heritage.

A self-described avid collector, Krystal then filled the space with loads of vintage finds and seemingly endless works of art—positioned, on occasion, in front of one of the home's massive windows. "I like hanging art in unexpected places. It frames out a space," says the designer. Statement-making accents such as a fireplace mantel and gilt chandelier came from other homes in the area by way of Facebook Marketplace. The result is a master class in reviving a historic property—and you can still see the seams, she says, where it was split for the move.

(LEFT) An antique barn door was put on a slider to create an entry to the en suite bath. *Bed:* AllModern. *Mirror:* Uttermost. *Bedside table:* Revelation. *Bedding:* Pottery Barn (throw), Target (duvet cover), vintage (shams). *Dresser:* vintage.

(ABOVE) Krystal sourced this mantel along with other elegant accents from a nearby renovation, then outfitted the bath with a heater to warm the marble room. *Carrara marble tiles:* The Home Depot. *Chandelier:* similar by Circa Lighting. *Table:* Uttermost. *Bath:* antique. *Faucets:* Moen.

NINA MAGON STUDIO
Houston

A couple's request for drama was met with touches of château chic.

Tasked with transforming a cookie-cutter spec home in Tanglewood, Texas, into a one-of-a-kind residence, Nina Magon of Houston-based Nina Magon Studio aimed for "harmonious sanctuary." But tranquility is tricky to achieve in a sprawling house.

Magon captured a serene energy by maintaining the same color palette throughout, with sleek furnishings seamlessly guiding the owners from room to room. "To break up all the hard lines and rectilinear profiles in the space, we featured curvaceous lounge chairs for our clients to retreat to," the designer says of a reading area in the primary bedroom. "These soft accents and light colors created the opportunity for the windows to be a striking focal point that allows the flow of natural light into the space." Textural finishes, such as a faux-wood plank vaulted ceiling that plays into the home's arches and exposed beams throughout, furthers the sense of timelessness.

Lively accents keep all this serenity from seeming sleepy. "Punctuated with bold details such as an organically shaped marble-and-brass coffee table, a vintage style glass chandelier, and curvilinear furniture, the living room intrigues and presents visual interest at every turn," she explains. The kitchen features architectural Ann Sacks tiles, the dining room walls are a rich finish, and countless custom pieces are designed by Magon: kitchen stools and cozy upholstered armchairs, the living room bookshelves, and more. Says the designer: "I want this space to be comforting and warm with a sense of sophisticated refinement."

(LEFT) Magon chose slate blue leather on the custom chairs in the dining room to pick up on the navy accents in the adjoining entry hall. *Walls:* plaster. *Table:* Cantoni. *Chandelier:* John-Richard Collection.

(PREVIOUS) A vintage-style glass chandelier by RH draws the eye upward, emphasizing an existing arched doorway and full-wall window. *Sofa:* Anthropologie, reupholstered by Nina Magon Studio. *Pink Chairs:* custom by Nina Magon Studio, manufactured by Creative Style Furniture. *Coffee table:* France & Son. *Artwork: La Fenêtre de L'Atelier à la Californie*, Pablo Picasso, via Off the Wall Gallery.

(PREVIOUS RIGHT) The primary bedroom took its design cues from large windows that flood the space with natural light and greenery. *Bedside table:* Made Goods.

With exposed wooden beams and a minimalist color scheme, the home's kitchen features custom stools by Nina Magon Studio. *Tile:* Ann Sacks. *Table:* RH. *Pendants:* Pottery Barn.

LIVE COLORFULLY

ABD STUDIO
Truckee, California

"You can literally leave from the back door and go on a forty-five-minute hike."

(LEFT) A custom bed frame incorporates a tufted headboard in the design. *Sconce:* Design Within Reach.

(RIGHT) "She loves the slightly bohemian and is such a visual person," Giannone says of her client. *Tub:* Blu Bathworks. *Fixtures:* Newport Brass. *Sconce:* Lumfardo Luminaires. *Rug:* vintage. *Cosmetic mirror:* The Line. *Stool at vanity:* Design Within Reach.

(PREVIOUS) The central focus of the main room is a Richard Misrach piece of a man floating in the water. "It evokes this serene feeling that Tahoe embodies for us, and it's one of my favorites," Claire says. *Pendant lights:* Frezoli Lighting. *Dining chairs:* Sawkille Co. *Dining table:* Nickey Kehoe. *Rug:* Armadillo.

Martis Camp, a private gated community near Truckee, California, backs up to the Tahoe National Forest. "You can literally leave from the back door and go on a forty-five-minute hike," says designer Brittany H. Giannone of ABD Studio. But when Claire and Holden Spaht hired Giannone to design a vacation home there, a typical forest cabin wasn't in order. Rather, they envisioned a sophisticated and modern but also laid-back getaway for them and their two teenage daughters—even if it was the kind of place where they might find a bear eating bacon straight from their refrigerator. (According to the designer, that really happened.)

Hewing to the community's strict architectural guidelines, Giannone maintained the cohesive feel of the modern homes throughout with nature-inspired elements like black-stained wood cladding, a stone facade, and a steely metal roof, but she differentiated the new-build house with activity-centered amenities she knew the family would appreciate, including a separate art studio, screened porch with a gas fireplace, and stainless steel hot tub.

Inside, the Spahts' collection of art and furniture lend a sense of contemporary flair The first piece they purchased for this home, a Richard Misrach photograph, set the watery palette—"It evokes this serene feeling that Tahoe embodies for us and it's one of my favorites," Claire says—while works by Kiki Smith, Tom McKinley, Sarah Sze, Luke Butler, Robert Mangold, Louise Bourgeois, Margo Wolowiec, and James Surls fill the walls. Even the housewares function as art. "Sometimes when clients ask for open shelves, they have a lot of clutter," says the designer, "but Claire is the type of person that even the mixing bowls are aesthetically pleasing."

Gray

(Mood Board)

(01)

Stately without being stale, warm without being white.

（03）

（04）

（01）Designer Jen Talbot added reverse-painted molding, dusty pink drapery, and bold berry chairs for full-on Parisian glam in this dining room. *Table:* Design Within Reach. *Chairs:* Interior Define. *Chandelier:* France & Son. （02）Grayscale furnishings and accessories impart depth in designer Anthony Dunning's black-and-white living room. *Pillows:* Celebrity Home (cross hatch), HW Home (zebra), Eastern Accents (trellis), Haute House Home (crushed velvet), Callisto Home (lumbar), Mr. Fantasy (eye print), Rodeo Home (silver). *Coffee table:* Phillips Collection. *Rug:* Ben Soleimani. （03）A butler's pantry by Andrea Goldman exudes a speakeasy vibe thanks to a Phillip Jeffries wallcovering. *Lamps and ceiling fixture:* Circa Lighting. *Stools:* Made Goods. （04）The team at ABD Studio chose a Lindsey Adelman chandelier and curtains in a Holly Hunt fabric to stand in relief against Benjamin Moore's Anchor Gray in this dining room. *Table:* Poliform. *Chairs:* vintage.

（05）

（06）

（07）

（05）A bedroom designed by Nannette Brown features a subtly textured plaster wall treatment by Benjamin Moore. *Wall art:* client's own. *Sconces:* vintage 1970s, Laurin Copen Antiques, with custom shades, Illumé. （06）Custom steel doors stream extra light into the living room of antiques dealers Stephen Abeles and Ray Attanasio. *Doors:* Soraya Osorio Ltd. *Wall paint:* mineral paint in 9008, Keim. *Rug:* custom, Doris Leslie Blau. （07）Jean Liu designed this custom cabinetry, coating it in Morris Room Grey by Sherwin-Williams for a warm finish. *Tables:* Mark Jupiter. *Chairs:* David Ericsson, Suite NY. *Banquette:* custom, in THEO leather, Kravet fabric. *Pendants:* Roman and Williams Guild. *Wine column:* Thermador.

(08)

(08) Bronze and other metallic accents keep the moody atmosphere from becoming cave-like in a living room
by Nannette Brown. *Paint:* Amherst Gray, Benjamin Moore. *Cocktail tables:* custom, Nannette Brown. *Rug:* ABC Carpet & Home.
Sconce: vintage, Barbara Barry for Circa Lighting.

(09)

(11)

(10)

(12)

(09) Nannette Brown installed a bright white banquette to offset the drama of this kitchen. *Tile:* Waterworks. *Pendants:* Rejuvenation. *Chairs:* Crate & Barrel. (10) Warm blue accents soften the modern lines of a bedroom by designer Jean Liu. (11) For a budget-friendly kitchen overhaul, designer Anne Sage went sleek with dark cabinetry from BOXI by Semihandmade. *Tile:* Fireclay Tile. *Appliances:* Samsung. *Sconce:* vintage Louis Poulsen. *Chairs:* vintage. (12) In this primary bedroom by designer Rodney Lawrence, LED strips make Lucite shelves look lit from within. *Paint:* Decorator's White, Benjamin Moore. *Wallcovering:* Wolf-Gordon. *Art:* Cecily Brown. (13) Designer Crystal Sinclair highlighted this banquette using crisp picture-frame molding. *Paint:* Metropolitan, Benjamin Moore. *Pendant:* Lambert & Fils. *Table:* Meadow Blu. *Banquette:* Stitchroom. (14) In the living room, Sinclair paired vintage and new pieces in a streamlined palette. *Sofa:* RH. *Chandelier:* Serge Mouille.

(13)

(14)

5 DESIGNER-APPROVED
Gray Paints
—

"Benjamin Moore
Onyx is dark and moody
and lets the surroundings
and glass expanse
really pop."

—

SARA CUKERBAUM,
principal of
SLIC Design

"Clare paint has the
best names. Penthouse
is a calm, medium
gray but hints at
something elevated, even
aspirational."

—

RAYMAN BOOZER,
principal of *Apartment 48*

"An earthy hue that
walks the line between
gray and green, C2 Paint
Carbon Dust feels both
historic and fresh."

—

KRISTEN EKELAND,
principal of
Studio Gild

"I chose Mist by The Paint
Laboratory for latticework
in a sunroom, and it
perfectly complemented
the greenery both inside
and out."

—

MIA JUNG,
interiors director for
Ike Kligerman Barkley

"I love Farrow & Ball
Ammonite. It's the perfect
neutral with a touch of
gray that works well in a
room on its own or with
white trim."

—

KELLY MCGUILL,
principal of
Kelly McGuill Home

LIVE COLORFULLY

Jewel Tones

Who needs diamonds? In these gem-inspired rooms, moody shades of SATURATED COLOR combine with rich textures. The result is always sophisticated and never soft-spoken.

ELIZABETH COOPER INTERIOR DESIGN
New York City

Cobalt. Deep sea. Sapphire.
This apartment uses every possible oceanic hue.

A cozy cocoon. That's the vision interior designer Elizabeth Cooper had for one family of four's prewar apartment, located on Manhattan's Upper East Side. "Because the family spends most of the summer at their house on Long Island and lives in New York City from the fall through the spring, we decided to make quite a bit of the color palette and materials a little richer—velvets, wool flannels, deep blues and greens, and chocolate brown, et cetera," she explains.

One color in particular became central to her scheme: "As we kept going, I was drawn more and more to the blues," Cooper recalls. Inky de Gournay Temple Newsam panels ("absolutely the single largest investment of time and detailed effort in this project") turn the entryway into a snowy woodland scene. The designer painted the interior doorways in Fine Paints of Europe Zuider Zee Blue, matched to the background color of the panels, to carry the feeling throughout the apartment.

Given that blue is a color that can come across as icy, the palette choice is somewhat of a surprise. But "when you get into deeper-colored blues, it becomes warmer," says Cooper, who intentionally paired robust indigos and navies with comforting upholstery.

As the daughter of a painter and sculptor, Cooper is highly attuned to the emotions certain tones can evoke. "I think that color is such a meaningful factor in a home, resonating with clients and making them happy," she says.

Where some designers might push clients to adopt a risky palette, Cooper would instead "encourage a decorative pillow in a color that's outside their comfort zone, but definitely make it a priority to surround homeowners in spaces that are filled with their favorite colors." The pink coffee table, the orange kumquats on a topiary tree in the living room—these are just glimmers of spring in a wintry wonderland.

—

(ABOVE) A pale gray vanity picks up blues in the dramatic Arabescato marble on the walls and countertop. *Paint:* custom, Elizabeth Cooper Interior Design. *Sconces:* The Urban Electric Co. *Medicine cabinet:* RH. *Sink and faucet:* Waterworks. *Vanity:* custom, Elizabeth Cooper Interior Design, fabricated by Steadfast Interiors.

(RIGHT) The library is a place where Cooper envisioned the family gathering to "watch movies, read, and spend time together." *Paint:* S 4005–B20G, Fine Paints of Europe. *Sconce:* Galerie des Lampes, Iatesta Studio, with custom silk shades. *Art:* Hunt Slonem. *Chair:* Howe London, in Penny Morrison fabric. *Sofa:* George Sherlock, in Holland & Sherry wool flannel. *Pillows:* Soane Britain (white floral) and Penny Morrison (dusty rose). *Curtain fabric:* Holland & Sherry, with Samuel & Sons trim.

LIVE COLORFULLY

LIVE COLORFULLY

NICK OLSEN INC.
New York City

How do you cure a cold, contemporary home?
Hire a whimsy-loving designer and let him loose.

"They don't like anything too formal or fussy with a capital F."

"Doesn't it look like you're at the bottom of a crystal-clear ocean?" asks Nick Olsen of the glistening baby blue he selected for a client's living-room ceiling. "I lobbied hard for that. The walls had this off-white creamy color with a pink undertone, so I just knew it would work." Such is the killer instinct—and infectious energy—of a designer making a name for himself by working bold colors into just about every project he undertakes. And not just for the fun of it.

Take that blue ceiling, which unites a quirky mix of furnishings and bounces daylight from tall windows to the far side of a 40-foot room. "They're definitely not afraid of color," says Olsen of the homeowners, a couple with three kids who commissioned him to infuse life into their 3,540-square-foot contemporary Manhattan town house. There were, of course, parameters. The home's sheetrock walls and open floor plan would require a certain amount of ingenuity to warm up. However, "she didn't want intense color in every room," says Olsen of the wife. With so many open, public spaces not clearly defined by partitions or doorways, Olsen couldn't cover every wall in bold hues. "I didn't want it to feel enclosed or encumbered," he says. So he created thoughtful chromatic zones throughout, guided by one particularly useful

purchase. "It all started with the carpet. It's the literal foundation of the entire house. I had some schemes worked up, but I tweaked everything when I found the pale aquamarine–and–Nantucket red Oushak carpet," he recalls.

In the open living-and-dining room with the blue ceiling, where the carpet resides, furniture with eclectic origins seem to be plucked directly from its color scheme: a French, neoclassical–inspired limed oak desk, a B&B Italia chaise covered in a coral Colefax and Fowler linen, a custom tufted sofa by Luther Quintana Upholstery in blue velvet, plus various side tables, pillows, and vibrantly colored contemporary art.

The same playful elegance pervades the rest of the house. In a children's bedroom, lemon yellow ceiling stripes recall parasols in the summer sun, and Scalamandré's playful La Fenêtre Ouverte fabric (translation: "the open window") is a fitting addition to twin beds. In the den, which doubles as guest quarters, a bamboo wallcovering is paired with a cushy green linen-velvet daybed and a Japanese folding screen purchased at auction. "This is a sophisticated house, but it also has an ease about it," Olsen says. "They don't like anything too formal or fussy with a capital F."

—

chairs mimic the sheen of a lacquered ceiling by Agustin Hurtado; matte details, like the Stephen Antonson chandelier and Lucca Studio sideboard, balance this finish. *Art: My Happiness*, by Sara Genn (large); *Trust and Love*, by Katy Ferrarone (small pair). *Chairs:* custom, Luther Quintana, in coral Global Leathers. *Table:* Theodore Alexander, hand-painted by Agustin Hurtado. *Lamp:* vintage. *Sideboard:* Lucca Studio. *Chandelier:* Stephen Antonson, Liz O'Brien.

saturated color in the room where the family gathers for Netflix sessions. A jade-green bamboo wallcovering by Kravet lends a cocooning effect. *Lampshades:* Gracious Home. *Daybed:* custom, Charles H. Beckley, in Pierre Frey linen velvet. *Pillows:* David Haag, in Malabar, Hines (stripe) and Pierre Frey Le Grand Corail (lumbar). *Table:* 1930s French, Naga base with a Built By Steel top painted in a faux marble finish by Christopher Pearson. *Chair:* Oscar de la Renta for Century Furniture, in Global Leather. *Carpet:* Sacco.

(LEFT) This antique aqua-and-red Oushak rug informed the whole apartment's color scheme. *Mirror:* vintage. *Chairs:* vintage, Gio Ponti for Isa Bergamo. *Chaise:* B&B Italia, upholstered in Colefax and Fowler. *Desk:* Built By Steel. *Art:* Jean-Marc Louis, Alexis England.

(FOLLOWING LEFT) "The twin daughters have very lively personalities, and I wanted their room to reflect that," says Olsen. So he chose a reissue of a cheery midcentury Paule Marrot print to upholster the custom Charles H. Beckley beds. *Ceiling:* custom finish by Christopher Pearson, using Bold Yellow and Super White, both by Benjamin Moore. *Wall paint:* Benjamin Moore Crystal Springs. *Pink blankets:* Kalyana Textiles. *Fabric on bed:* Scalamandré. *Pillows:* custom, in Clarence House fabric. *Art:* Hans Meyer Petersen. *Mirror:* custom.

(FOLLOWING RIGHT) Patterned throw pillows in a Schumacher fabric pop against the T. H. Robsjohn-Gibbings–style sectional in the eat-in kitchen. *Sofa:* custom by Luther Quintana Upholstery, in a Pollack vinyl. *Teal lumbar pillow:* Crate & Barrel. *Sconces:* Donghia. *Garden seat:* John Rosselli & Associates. *Rug:* antique, from Bazar Oriental Rugs..

213

KATI CURTIS DESIGN
Brookline, Massachusetts

Creative thinking gives a cramped Tudor colorful new life.

"I want no white walls." That was the first directive Kati Curtis's clients gave when she began work on their 1930s Tudor in Brookline, Massachusetts (which Curtis found on Zillow and "convinced them to buy"). "That," says the pattern-loving designer, "was music to my ears!" One hitch: The home's original layout didn't allow in much light, which could have caused a color-rich scheme to feel claustrophobic.

"It was a very inward-looking building," explains architect J. B. Clancy of ART Architects, who was hired to help give the home a more modern flow, "and it was cut up into tons of little spaces with no access to the outside." Curtis and Clancy came up with an unconventional solution, carving out a central stairwell above the entryway. "The rest of the rooms became more intimate spaces around this central hub," explains Clancy.

Curtis outfitted the surrounding rooms in rich jewel tones and layered vintage furniture and textiles that add depth to the client's colorful art collection. High-gloss finishes give room after room a polished look, and help bounce light into every corner. Curtis worked closely with Clancy and a team of artisans to perfect textural details like wood beams and wrought-iron trim, which add a necessary edge to a style Curtis refers to as "Millennial Gothic."

In addition to the light well, the new layout features a number of useful rooms rather than an open floor plan: "The house is actually quite small, so we had to carve out a lot of different areas," says Curtis, who considered how the family's needs might evolve when designating purposes. One space, in red lacquer, is presently a playroom for the family's two young children, "but could one day turn into a dining room," the designer points out. Now that's planning ahead.

LIVE COLORFULLY

Curtis devised a rich custom green from Fine Paints of Europe for the kitchen cabinetry. *Range:* Wolf. *Counter stools:* Lee Industries, in Perennials fabric. *Backsplash:* FLM Ceramics. *Faucets:* Brizo. *Pendants:* Circa Lighting. *Countertops:* quartzite.

FLAWLESS
High Gloss
—

Achieving the perfect mirror-like sheen isn't for the faint of heart. "It's a very labor-intensive process," says designer Kati Curtis of the meticulous work, which requires a professional painter and lots of time for sanding, painting, and drying between multiple layers. Even the slightest bump or wrinkle will show if the application isn't flawless. But it's a great way to "give a room depth and light reflection," she says. If you decide to go for it, choose an alkyd-based paint to impart what she calls a "true gloss finish." (Note: this paint isn't removable.) For just a bit of shine, you can use high-gloss water-based paints, which can be low VOC and dry faster.

221

A second-floor landing with two cozy chairs is accessed by crossing a bridge that extends over the stairwell. *Wallpaper:* Josef Frank, Schumacher. *Curtains:* Clare Louise Frost. *Rug:* Landry & Arcari. *Chairs:* Lee Industries, upholstered in Carolina Irving (blue) and Tulu Textiles (red) fabrics.

LIVE COLORFULLY

PETER DUNHAM & ASSOCIATES
Southampton, New York

"You don't really see where the sea ends and your room begins."

After looking at nearly 60 homes in Southampton, New York, Peter Dunham's clients went big. Perched on a cliff overlooking glimmering Shinnecock Bay, the 8,800-square-foot, 7-bedroom, 9-bath house had space to spare and a near flawless setting. But being a spec house, the architecture was pretty much entirely devoid of soul.

In came Dunham, the France-born, England-trained prince of patterned prints. "You need to layer in some personality. You have to give spaces their identity," he explains. Dunham began by sheathing much of the interior in Benjamin Moore's Simply White ("it's clean, it's airy, it's bright"). Key rooms, on the other hand, received a colorful treatment: "You're looking for ways to vary the notes so the whole house is not blue and white." The designer installed a real wood wallcovering—de facto planking—in the den, and custom blue milk paint in the downstairs guest bedroom.

Because the clients have grandchildren, they asked for fuss-free, hard-wearing materials. Dunham selected performance fabrics and bold antique carpets that could take a beating (because they already had—for decades). Throughout, abundant pattern cuts any sameness. But how do you mix prints without summoning a dizzy spell? "It's a balance, almost like cooking, the way you have a rich sauce next to a plain piece of fish," Dunham says. "I'll add something like a paisley with stripes and then throw some solid in with the trim."

The final effect is as lively and deep as the bay beyond the windows. "To me, the atmosphere is way more important than the look," Dunham says. "You don't want guests to feel intimidated by your 10,000-square-foot house on the water. It should feel like they can kick off their shoes."

"You need to layer in some personality. You have to give spaces their identity."

"Orange is a great color that's not hot like red," says Dunham, who added a tiny bit as trim on the window treatments to play off the sofa. *Wallcovering:* Nobilis. *Sofa, pillows, and ottoman:* Hollywood at Home (sofa in a Pindler fabric and ottoman in vintage textile). *Floor poufs:* Mecox. *Window shades:* Pindler.

229

CECILIA CASAGRANDE INTERIORS
Brookline, Massachusetts

There's no shortage of wild wallcoverings
and vintage treasures in this sun-drenched home.

(PREVIOUS) The shelves are curated with a selection of books, heirlooms, and mementos from the couple's travels. "The monkey is hand-painted by artisans in Oaxaca, Mexico. It takes six months for one artisan to make!" says Casagrande. *Sofa:* Dune. *Sconces:* DelightFULL.

(LEFT) The designer wanted the kitchen to feel like a Parisian bistro. *Chandelier:* Lindsey Adelman. *Sconces:* Atelier de Troupe. *Hood and sink:* custom, Vogler Metalwork & Design. *Pendant light:* Allied Maker. *Wallpaper:* Dark Floral, Ellie Cashman. *Table:* Sean Woolsey Studio. *Chairs:* Saarinen Executive. *Stools:* De La Espada. *Faucet:* Barber Wilsons & Co.

Frigid Boston winters aren't known for their feel-good vibes, but Cecilia Casagrande and her husband can't help but smile through them. Much of that has to do with the large south-facing windows that let as much light into their four-story, 1872 Victorian home in Brookline, Massachusetts, as possible—"It's glorious sun all day long inside this house," she explains. But it's also a result of the very intentional palette Casagrande concepted from the get-go.

"I wanted all of my rooms to sing and be a joy to spend time in, to have a beating heart that was artful and rich," she remembers. She also knew that color could be an antidote to a long season of hibernation. "The Boston winters and spring are very white outside—it takes a while for the green leaves to come out on the trees, so that's why the color palettes for all of the rooms have rich, saturated tones. They all connect and have a gentle flow."

She describes the deep Farrow & Ball Hague Blue–clad living room as a jewel box—"sexy, dark, and vibrant." Inspired by a French bistro, the kitchen takes a fresher traditional-meets-modern approach with hand-crafted tiles, brown grout, marble countertops, and an unlacquered brass faucet and sink to add warmth to the room. She calls the primary bedroom, with its dark Studio Green walls, also by Farrow & Ball, "soothing and cozy."

The designer kept her roots in mind when conceptualizing the formal living room. "I grew up going to England every year—my father is British—so I wanted a bit of that royal feel. I love the vibrant colors of British design that keep up the spirits during those oh so many gray days." While one of the brass chests flanking the original fireplace was a gift from her parents, the other (an exact match!) was found at the Brimfield Antiques Flea Market. The shelves are curated with a selection of books, heirlooms (like her grandmother's Louis Vuitton Speedy bag), and mementos from the couple's travels. No matter the weather in Boston, it's always sunny inside this house.

(PREVIOUS) Society Limonta bedding jives with rich Studio Green by Farrow & Ball walls. *Sconces:* Schoolhouse. *Side tables:* Peter Deeble.

(RIGHT) "I channeled my English roots—down to the English brand of paints I used," says Casagrande of Farrow & Ball Hague Blue on the walls of the living room. "I chose a jewel box color palette for my living room: sexy, dark, and vibrant."

1 PAINT,
Four Lights
—

How FARROW & BALL Hague Blue reads in four different parts of this home.

236

LILLY BUNN INTERIORS
Locust Valley, New York

A personal mix and just the right paints revive
a 1930s getaway in record time.

"It was just the sweetest little cottage," says Lilly Bunn of the Locust Valley home she and her family bought as a weekend getaway—and rehabbed in just a month. In record time, she spruced up the 1930s house with jolts of color and personal touches without detracting from the original bones. "The way I decorate for myself is that I like everything to feel serendipitous," Bunn says. "A lot of the things in this house I had found and gathered already. I just brought in all the things I liked and got it all done."

The faux-bois wallcovering "made it feel cottagey immediately," says Bunn, who decided to leave the windows bare, a tactic that saved time and showed off the original details. "In these old houses, if you just paint the windows, it solves any problems," Bunn says. She added texture with custom lampshades made from saris bought on Etsy. "In my office there are just tons of boxes of them, and every time we do a project we just shop from there, just pull up whatever colors work."

Given the home's relatively small square footage, Bunn wanted every last inch to count. That meant carving a room out of the existing stairwell. "We put carpeting down and we painted it; we wanted it to feel cozy," she says. "The ceilings aren't that high, but it's fun for the kids to hang out there—it's kind of like a cozy nook for them."

"When you have a low-ceilinged cottage like this, it's great to use dark colors," advises Bunn. "It gives it that cozy kind of English feel, and I love the way the moody blue gets shadowy and how it looks with the green of the trees outside."

(PREVIOUS AND RIGHT) By painting the old window frames a dark green, Bunn gave the 1930s architecture a distinctively fresh upgrade. *Paint:* Palmer Green, Benjamin Moore. *Sofas:* Tiger Furniture (light gray), in Rogers & Goffigon fabric; vintage (green pattern), in Colefax and Fowler chintz. *Slipper chairs:* vintage, in Muriel Brandolini printed cotton. *Red pillows:* Scalamandré silk velvet. *Rug:* custom, Beauvais. *Coffee table:* Lillian August. *Art:* Framebridge.

238

"When you have a low-ceilinged cottage like this, it's great to use dark colors," advises Bunn. "It gives it that cozy kind of English feel." *Headboard:* Serena & Lily. *Bedding:* Biscuit Home. *Lamp:* Pottery Barn. *Nightstand:* Chelsea Additions. *Art:* Jane Bunn.

(RIGHT) "We weren't planning to do much formal entertaining," Bunn says, "so we opened the dining room up to the kitchen." She painted it a fun mint color and furnished the space with a table and chairs from Ballard Designs—in stock for quick shipping. *Paint:* for similar try Kittery Point Green, Benjamin Moore. *Pendant:* vintage. *Chairs:* Ballard Designs. *Table:* Miles Redd for Ballard Designs. *Rug:* Beauvais. *Art:* Lulie Wallace.

"The proportions of the rooms were just perfect, so there was really nothing to do but paint."

COREY DAMEN JENKINS & ASSOCIATES
Michigan

One designer's gift for diplomatic compromise
results in a home that perfectly marries two distinct styles.

(PREVIOUS) A Phillip Jeffries lacquered wallcovering is a smart choice for spaces that get a lot of use, like this "flex room" where the kids do homework. "If someone draws on it, it's a lot easier to repair than real lacquer!" says Jenkins. *Chandelier:* Arteriors. *Lamps:* Currey & Company. *Art:* Cloth & Kind. *Credenza:* clients' own. *Curtains:* Kravet. *Table:* Mercury Row. *Chairs:* Langley Street. *Rug:* West Elm.

(LEFT) PPG Paint in Garlic Clove has enough warmth to counterbalance the bright white of the often snowy landscape. *Chandeliers:* Arteriors (left), The Urban Electric Co. (right). *Sofa:* custom. *Chairs:* Hickory Chair. *Cocktail table:* RH. *Rug:* Stark. *Dining table:* Design Within Reach. *Dining chairs:* Bernhardt. *Ceiling paint:* Revere Pewter, Benjamin Moore.

If Corey Damen Jenkins weren't an interior designer, he'd probably be working in fashion or running for political office—"my other great loves!" he says. After all, it was both a couture-level attention to detail and statesmanlike approach that made his recent project for a Michigan family a success.

The homeowners, who were in the early stages of building a new house, contacted Jenkins after seeing his colorful, neotraditional work in a magazine. "They'd gone on my website and watched my videos," he recalls. "They told me, 'We like you as a person, but can you do something that's more streamlined and modern?'"

"I was actually grateful to not do something super-traditional!" the designer admits. The real challenge, he discovered after meeting the couple, would be in marrying their "very disparate" aesthetic points of view. "The wife loved jewel tones and embellishment, while the husband was on the total opposite end of the spectrum—no color, no wallpaper, no window treatments," Jenkins explains. "The question was, how do you bring those things together in a way that feels cohesive?"

The answer: serious negotiations. "I'd do a clean-lined sofa for him, but in an emerald green velvet for her. Then she'd want nailhead trim, which seemed too traditional to him, so we'd do it in polished chrome, which made it modern," he recalls. "It was a tug-of-war, but it was fun!"

Those sorts of creative compromises abound throughout the house. To appease the husband's aversion to window treatments—without sacrificing privacy—Jenkins installed motorized blinds that are concealed against the window frame when not in use. The decorative molding in the living room is a flat stock instead of ogee, so it feels geometric instead of fussy. And when the wife asked for classic panels in the dining room, Jenkins obliged but in a 1970s-inspired grass cloth with a mod chandelier.

Jenkins's aesthetic is visible in the finished home, but it's his clients' personalities that shine through. "I always say that I approach design like a doctor delivering a baby: At the end of the day, it's not my kid—it's yours, and it should look like you," he laughs. "After all, you're the ones taking it home!"

(ABOVE) "With all the white walls and 18-foot ceilings, I was able to get away with bringing in some bold wallcoverings," says Jenkins, who chose a graphic Phillip Jeffries pattern for a cozy niche off of the foyer. *Art and table:* Cloth & Kind. *Bench:* Kravet. *Pillow fabrics:* Schumacher.

(RIGHT) "You see this room as soon as you walk in, so I used it as an opportunity to introduce the palette in a strong way," Jenkins says. *Ceiling and wallcovering:* Kravet. *Chandelier:* Circa Lighting. *Table:* Caracole. *Armchairs:* Hickory Chair in a GP&J Baker fabric. *Side chairs:* Hickory Chair. *Roman shade:* Kravet (fabric) and Robert Allen (trim).

Green

(01)

As vibrant and life-giving as the rooms they distinguish.

(02)

(03)

(04)

(05)

(01) A herringbone backsplash exudes earthy elegance in this timeless kitchen designed by Ginny Macdonald. *Paint:* Doric White (back cabinets) and Courtyard Green (foreground cabinets), both Dunn Edwards. *Tile:* Sonoma Tilemakers. (02) A refreshing green-and-blue palette maximizes productivity in a laundry room by Courtnay Tartt Elias of Creative Tonic. *Paints:* Meditative (blue) and Snowbound (white), both by Sherwin-Williams. *Wall tiles:* Crossville. (03) To pep up this powder room, Elizabeth Lawrence of Bunny Williams Interior Design chose a vibrant Paper Mills wallcovering. *Pendant:* Shades of Light. *Sconce:* Circa Lighting. *Mirror:* Michael S. Smith for Mirror Home. *Sink:* Urban Archaeology. *Faucet:* Waterworks. (04) To make her breakfast nook feel more intimate, Stephanie Bradshaw covered the walls in Studio Green by Farrow & Ball. *Pendant:* Currey & Company. *Chairs:* CB2. *Bench:* custom, in a Schumacher fabric with pillows in fabrics from Mokum and Cowtan & Tout. (05) Kemble Interiors founder Mimi McMakin reinvented a traditional Palm Beach library by painting over the brown built-in millwork with a custom sage-green glaze, made by mixing green, blue, raw umber and black Universal Tints, which was then added to a Benjamin Moore oil-glazing liquid.

(08)

(09)

(06)

(07)

(06) A Kravet grasscloth in the back of built-in bookcases painted in Stillwater by Benjamin Moore channels the vivid green of the Schumacher drapery in this living room by Courtnay Tartt Elias of Creative Tonic. *Chairs:* custom by the Joseph Company, in a Vervain velvet. *Coffee table:* Area.
(07) A poolhouse by Chloe Warner of Redmond Aldrich Design summons vacation vibes with the original Martinique banana leaf–themed wallpaper by CW Stockwell. (08) A glossy green pantry by Creative Tonic balances traditional and contemporary elements. *Paint:* Shamrock, Sherwin-Williams. Tile: Pomogranit/ADR. *Shade:* fabric by S. Harris Vivier. *Lighting:* Urban Electric. (09) Designer Cynthia Collins converted a coat closet into a glamorous home bar using celadon Waterhouse Wallhangings wallpaper. *Settee:* custom, in Pierre Frey fabric. *Chest:* antique.

(10)

(10) Designer Lindsay Rhodes covered the walls, ceiling, and cabinets of this bar area in a pistachio hue that pulls from the green-veined marble countertops.

5 DESIGNER-APPROVED
Green Paints

—

"Sherwin-Williams Shamrock is a clear winner when it comes to bringing the Amazonian freshness of nature into the midst of an urban jungle."

—

JUAN CARRETERO, principal of *Capital C Interiors*

"We love Mediterranean Olive by Benjamin Moore. We've used this on both walls and millwork, and in different sheens."

—

DAN MAZZARINI, principal of *BHDM Design*

"Path by C2 Paint is a chameleon of sorts, the perfect sophisticated mix of blue and green that goes in either direction."

—

JULIE ROOTES, principal of *Julie Rootes Interiors*

"Secret Garden by Dulux brings the outdoors inside, creating a naturalistic and soothing environment."

—

JEFFREY A. WILKES, founder and principal of *DesignWilkes*

"Benjamin Moore's Huntington Green is one of my favorite accents when a room is begging for a bold punch of color. "

—

EMILY JUNE SPANOS, principal of *Emily June Design*

(11)

(12)

(13)

(14)

(15)

(11) Farrow & Ball Breakfast Room Green establishes a serene backdrop for an ornate Lee Jofa drapery fabric, care of designer Mark D. Sikes. *Wallcoverings:* custom, Adelphi Paper Hangings. *Desk:* Soane Britain. Rug: Stark. Chandelier: Hudson Valley Lighting. (12) "When you're in the shower and look up, you feel like you're in a jungle," says designer Amy Courtney of the Cole and Son wallcovering. *Artwork:* Alison Causer. *Sink:* IKEA.
(13) Highlighted by Benjamin Moore Lehigh Green on the walls, a Brunschwig & Fils fabric creates a sunny sitting area in Cynthia Collins's Dallas home.
(14) Gently sloped shelves keep this walk-in pantry by Alice Lane Interior Design from feeling overstuffed. *Pendant:* Circa Lighting. *Paint:* Dakota Woods Green, Benjamin Moore. (15) Designer Fitz Pullins finds the Cole and Son wallpaper he used for this primary bath both "entertaining" and "invigorating." *Vanities:* RH. *Chair:* Anthropologie. *Sconces:* Arteriors. *Rug:* Texere via Oasis Rug & Home.

CREDITS

(INTRODUCTION)
p.6: Designer: Nickey Kehoe. Photographer: Amy Neunsinger. Producer: Robert Rufino. Paint: Studio Green, Farrow & Ball. Art: Michael Abrams, Sears Peyton Gallery. Sofa: custom in Libeco Fabric. Pillows: Pat McGann, Nickey Kehoe Shop. Ottoman: custom, in Jennifer Shorto for Harbinger. Chair: Nickey Kehoe Shop in Claremont fabric. Side table: Counter Space LA. Sconces: Obsolete. Rug: Marc Phillips.

(EARTH TONES)
p.8: Designer: Kathleen Walsh Interiors. Table: Pilar Proffitt, Ralph Pucci International. Chandelier: Pouenat, Holly Hunt. Rug: vintage. Corner chair: antique, covered in Lee Jofa. Pillow fabrics: Osborne & Little (pink) and Clarence House (multicolor and blue) on sofa; Le Gracieux on chairs. Art: client's own.

pp.10–17: Studio Shamshiri. Writer: Sean Santiago. Photographer: Stephen Kent Johnson/Otto.

pp.18–25: Kureck Jones. Writer: Kathryn O'Shea-Evans. Photographer: Eric Piasecki/Otto. Producer: Robert Rufino.

pp.26–31: Ursino Interiors. Writer: Jennifer Fernandez. Photographer: Tim Lenz.

pp.32–39: Alexander Doherty Design. Writer: Jennifer Fernandez. Photographer: Marius Chira.

pp.40–45: Lauren Liess + Co. Writer: Kelly Allen. Photographer: Helen Norman. Producer: Robert Rufino.

pp.46–51: Halden Interiors. Writer: Hadley Keller. Photographer: Brittany Ambridge/Otto.

pp.52–57: Erin Sander Design. Writer: David Nash. Photographer: Nathan Schroder.

(MOOD BOARD: BLUE)
pp. 58–59: (01) Photographer: Jacob Snavely. (02) Photographer: Emily Followill. (03) Photographer: Lindsay Salazar. (04) Photographer: Read McKendree.

pp.60–61: (05) Photographer: Jared Kuzia. (06) Photographer: Katie Nixon. (07) Photographer: Meghan Beierle-O'Brien. (08) Photographer: Trevor Tondro. (09) Photographer: Colin Price.

pp.62–63: (10) Photographer: Noe Dewitt. (11) Photographer: Emily Followill. (12) Photographer: Colin Price. (13) Photographer: Julie Soefer.

(PRIMARY COLORS)
p.64: Designer: Phillip Thomas Inc. Photographer: Thomas Loof. Producer: Robert Rufino. Paint: Flash Gold, Modern Masters Metallics (ceiling); Ladybug Red, Benjamin Moore (walls). Sofa: custom, Phillip Thomas Inc., in Schumacher velvet with Samuel & Sons trim. Pillow fabric: Clarence House with Robert Allen trim (ikat); Hutton Home with Robert Allen trim (gold); Lee Jofa with Samuel & Sons trim (blue). Chairs: custom, Phillip Thomas Inc., in Scalamandré fabric with Samuel & Sons trim (yellow); custom, Phillip Thomas Inc., in Pierre Frey fabric with Samuel & Sons trim. Ottomans: custom, Phillip Thomas Inc., in Studioart leather. Art: Morning Walk Kenya by Christopher Gates Scott, Shingle Island Photography. Curtain fabric: Holly Hunt. Rug: Stark Carpet.

pp.66–71: Ore Studios. Writer: Hadley Mendelsohn. Photographer: Haris Kenjar. Producer: Robert Rufino.

pp.72–77: Mark D. Sikes. Writer: Hadley Keller. Photographer: Amy Neunsinger.

pp.78–83: Phillip Thomas Inc. Writer: Kaitlin Menza. Photographer: Thomas Loof. Producer: Robert Rufino.

pp.84–89: Lisa Stone Design. Writer: Mary Elizabeth Andriotis. Photographer: Reid Rolls.

pp.90–95: Ariene Bethea. Writer: Hadley Keller. Photographer: Brie Williams. Producer: Robert Rufino.

(MOOD BOARD: RED)
pp.96–97: (01) Photographer: Emily Followill. (02) Photographer: George Ross. (03) Photographer: Andrea Calo. (04) Photographer: Jessica Antola. (05) Photographer: Janet Mesic-Mackie.

pp.98–99: (06) Photographer: Thomas Loof/Trunk Archive. (07) Photographer: Bjorn Wallander. (08) Photographer: Nathan Schroder.

pp.100–101: (09) Photographer: Stephen Kent Johnson/Otto. (10) Photographer: Andrea Calo. (11) Photographer: Sarah Winchester. (12) Photographer: Angela Seckinger. (13) Photographer: Francesco Lagnese.

(PALE PASTELS)
p. 102: Designer: Melanie Turner Interiors. Photographer: Mali Azima. Paint: Windswept Canyon, Sherwin-Williams. Artwork: America Martin, TEW Galleries. Sconces and armchairs: vintage. Ottoman: Hickory Chair. Table: CB2. Large vase: Made Goods. Carpet: Miami Circle Floor Coverings. Bench: vintage in Scalamandré fabric.

pp.104–109: Barry Dixon. Writer: Kaitlin Menza. Photographer: Luke White. Producer: Doretta Sperduto.

pp.110–115: Caroline Rafferty Interiors. Writer: Emma Bazilian. Photographer: Thomas Loof. Producer: Robert Rufino.

pp.116–121: Janie Molster Designs. Writer: Amanda Sims Clifford. Photographer: Mali Azima. Producer: Robert Rufino.

pp.122–127: Sherrell Design Studio. Writer: Hadley Keller. Photographer: Cate Black.

pp.128–133: Ariel Okin Interiors. Writer: Hadley Keller. Photographer: Donna Dotan.

pp.134–139: Phoebe Howard. Writer: Kathryn O'Shea-Evans. Photographer: Noe Dewitt. Producer: Robert Rufino.

(MOOD BOARD: PINK)
pp.140–141: (01) Photographer: Space Content Studio. (02) Photographer: Kendall Mccaugherty. (03) Photographer: Read McKendree. (04) Photographer: Alex Zarour.

pp.142–143: (05) Photographer: Sean Litchfield. (06) Photographer: Laurey Glenn. (07) Photographer: Bjorn Wallander/Otto.

pp.144–145: (08) Photographer: Brittany Ambridge/Otto. (09) Photographer: Bjorn Wallander/Otto. (10) Photographer: Tyler Hogan. (11) Photographer: Jared Kuzia.

(WARM NEUTRALS)
pp.146: Designer: Nina Magon Studio. Photographer: Julie Soefer. Chairs: custom. Table: Cantoni. Chandelier: John-Richard Collection.

pp.148–153: M. Elle Design. Writer: Hadley Keller. Photographer: Shade Degges.

pp.154–161: Sean Anderson Design. Writer: Kelly Allen. Photographer: Haris Kenjar.

pp.162–169: Amber El-Amin. Writer: Lauren Jones. Photographer: Carley Summers.

pp.170–175: Jae Joo Designs. Writer: Nikhita Mahtani. Photographer: Shade Degges. Producer: Robert Rufino.

pp.176–181: Krystal Matthews Design. Writer: Hadley Mendelsohn. Photographer: Jessie Preza. Producer: Robert Rufino.

pp.182–187: Nina Magon Studio. Writer: Muriel Vega. Photographer: Julie Soefer. Producer: Robert Rufino.

pp.188–193: ABD Studio. Writer: Lauren Jones. Photographer: Suzanna Scott.

(MOOD BOARD: GRAY)
pp.194–195: (01) Photographer: Dustin Halleck. (02) Photographer: Winnie Au. (03) Photographer: Michael Robinson. (04) Photographer: Bess Friday.

pp.196–197: (05) Photographer: Chris Mottalini. (06) Photographer: Björn Wallander. (07) Photographer: Stephen Karlisch. (08) Photographer: Chris Mottalini.

pp.198–199: (09) Photographer: Chris Mottalini. (10) Photographer: Stephen Karlisch. (11) Photographer: Elizabeth Messina. (12) Photographer: Marili Forastieri. (13) Photographer: Sean Litchfield. (14) Photographer: Sean Litchfield.

(JEWEL TONES)
p.200: Designer: Right Meets Left Interior Design. Photographer: Frank Frances. Producer: Robert Rufino. Headboard: O. Henry House, in Jardin Des Reves Prisme by Christian Lacroix fabric, Osborne & Little. Paint: Colonial Verdigris, Benjamin Moore. Bolster fabric: Raspberry Parade, Makrosha. Blanket: Hunt Slonem. Lamp: Wildwood with a Broome Lampshades shade.

pp.202–207: Elizabeth Cooper Interior Design. Writer: Danielle Harling. Photographer: Read McKendree.

pp.208–215: Nick Olsen Inc. Writer: Jennifer Fernandez. Photographer: Thomas Loof. Producer: Robert Rufino.

pp.216–223: Kati Curtis Design. Writer: Hadley Keller. Photographer: Thomas Loof/ Trunk Archive. Producer: Robert Rufino.

pp.224–229: Peter Dunham & Associates. Writer: Kathryn O'Shea-Evans. Photographer: Annie Schlechter. Producer: Robert Rufino.

pp.230–235: Cecilia Casagrande Interiors. Writer: David Nash. Photographer: Sean Litchfield.

pp.236–241: Lilly Bunn Interiors. Writer: Hadley Keller. Photographer: Jacqueline Clair.

pp.242–247: Corey Damen Jenkins & Associates. Writer: Emma Bazilian. Photographer: Werner Straube. Producer: Robert Rufino. Stylist: Hilary Rose.

(MOOD BOARD: GREEN)
pp.248–249: (01) Photographer: Sara Ligorria-Tramp. (02) Photographer: Julie Soefer. (03) Photographer: Andrew Frasz. (04) Photographer: Stacy Zarin Goldberg. (05) Photographer: Carmel Brantley.

pp.250–251: (06) Photographer: Julie Soefer. (07) Photographer: Bess Friday. (08) Photographer: Nathan Schroder. (09) Photographer: Julie Soefer. (10) Photographer: Alyssa Rosenheck.

pp.252–253: (11) Photographer: Amy Neunsinger. (12) Photographer: Sean Litchfield. (13) Photographer: Nathan Schroder. (14) Photographer: Joe Schmelzer. (15) Photographer: Jessie Preza.

For Abrams:
Editor: Rebecca Kaplan
Design: Alex Hunting Studio
Design Manager: Danielle Youngsmith
Managing Editor: Lisa Silverman
Production Manager: Kathleen Gaffney

For *House Beautiful*:
Editorial Director: Joanna Saltz
Executive Editor: Amanda Sims Clifford
Creative Director: Marc Davila
Director of Content Operations: Lindsey Ramsey
Director of Editorial Special Projects:
Carisha Swanson
Senior Style Director: Robert Rufino
Digital Director: Hadley Keller
Senior Editors: Emma Bazilian, Hadley
Mendelsohn, Kristin Tablang
Senior Editor of Content Strategy: Nathalie
Kirby
Associate Editor: Mary Elizabeth Andriotis
Associate Shopping Editors: Kelly Allen,
Medgina Saint-Elien
Contributing Project Editor: Jennifer Fernandez
Contributing Editors: Danielle Harling, Elzy Kolb,
Tiffany Ma, Jill Malter, Kaitlin Menza, Siobhán
McGowan, Monica Mercuri, Carly Olson, Kathryn
O'Shea Evans, Sara Rodrigues.
Art Director: Jee Lee
Deputy Art Director: Alice Morgan
Chief Visual Content Director,
Hearst Magazines: Alix Campbell
Executive Visual Director: Christina Weber
Deputy Visual Directors: Allison Chin,
Don Kinsella
Senior Visual Editor: Jillian Sellers
Visual Production Coordinators: Sabrina Toto,
Emilie Benyowitz